A KIND OF SLEEPWALKING

With love
from Dot. x

Praise for *A Kind of Sleepwalking*:

'This brief but beautiful book conveys a profound message in a wonderfully accessible way. Searingly honest personal reflection combines with a wide range of poems and quotations to illuminate several well-known stories from the Bible. It has challenged me to "wake-up" – and helped me to take a fresh look beneath the surface of my life.'

James Newcome, Bishop of Carlisle

'Judy Hirst draws compassionately on her varied experience as priest, mother, teacher, counsellor and friend to demonstrate how God gently wakes us from the long, lazy sleep of twenty-first century living and offers us far more exhilarating encounters with the reality of God and of ourselves. An honest, personal and moving book to enrich our faith journey.'

John Pritchard, Bishop of Oxford

'Judy Hirst's new book is a rare combination of personal experience and spiritual reflection. As many readers already know, she has a particular gift for writing with both clarity and honesty. *A Kind of Sleepwalking* does not subject us to shocks and alarms; rather it gently entices us to awake to a new quality of human and Christian living. I warmly commend it.'

Michael Sadgrove, Dean of Durham

'This is a wise and wonderful book: challenging and life-affirming but also funny and very moving. Judy Hirst leads us by the hand through the landscape of human life, gently pointing out all we miss as we sleepwalk our way through this busy world.'

Baroness Maeve Sherlock

'*A Kind of Sleepwalking* opens our eyes to an often unseen truth: that we tend to go through life without experiencing it in its fullness. With sensitivity, humour, biblical example, anecdote and huge doses of realism, Judy Hirst helps us to recognise when the realities of life might break in and wake us up but also challenges us to see them, even the most difficult situations, as opportunities for growth.'

Caroline Welby

A KIND OF
SLEEPWALKING

... and waking up to life

JUDY HIRST

DARTON · LONGMAN + TODD

To my mother and father, Jean and Claude;
who gave me life and taught me to love.

First published in Great Britain in 2014 by
Darton, Longman and Todd Ltd
1 Spencer Court
140 – 142 Wandsworth High Street
London SW18 4JJ

ISBN 978-0-232-52887-0

A catalogue record for this book is available from the British Library

Designed and phototypeset by Judy Linard
Printed and bound in Great Britain, by Bell & Bain, Glasgow

CONTENTS

FOREWORD
by Steven Croft, Bishop of Sheffield

Every so often, I'm in a meeting where someone falls asleep. It's usually a dull meeting in the early afternoon after a good lunch. The agenda or the speaker drones on. The head nods, the eyelids close, the breathing becomes deeper and more even and just occasionally a little louder. Usually everyone around looks on the person with kindness – just so long as they are not speaking or chairing the meeting (or snoring too loudly).

A nap in the early afternoon is one thing but sleepwalking through life is quite another. As Judy describes this kind of sleepwalking here it is a kind of drifting through life rather than living abundantly, going through the motions rather than experiencing all that God has to give to us.

We can sleepwalk at many different stages of our lives and I believe this book will be helpful to all kinds and ages of people. Young adults drift through their twenties or thirties, postponing life's key decisions and waiting for responsibility and real life to begin. In midlife, people who are under pressure in work and family life sleepwalk in a different way: we can ignore the really important things because we are on a treadmill. The years simply pass us by. In later life, our minds and senses easily become dull: we become uncritical consumers, our hearts and consciences are hardened, we no longer hear the voice of God and we grow into less than we could be.

Judy Hirst writes with love and compassion, with humanity and grace and good humour. She invites us, very gently but very

6

firmly, to wake up and stop dreaming our way through life. We are invited to rediscover the whole tapestry of human living, suffering and wonder, life and death, and most of all, love which calls us and renews us. The book is more like a gentle tap on the shoulder and the offer of a cup of coffee than a bucket of cold water. But it is a call to wake up nonetheless and an invitation to live life more deeply, with greater adventure, with greater love.

Judy and I were good colleagues some years ago and we have remained good friends. I know therefore that this book has emerged from the experience of many thousands of conversations, from a life well lived, from many friendships, from sermons and retreats, from suffering and laughter and from much prayer. I know too that Judy does not find the discipline of writing easy (though I believe it is something she does extremely well). Like her earlier book, *Struggling to be Holy*, *A Kind of Sleepwalking* is like a very good wine: rich, authentic and full of good things, a book to read slowly and return to and savour.

You will find many good things here in life's joys and, I hope, helpful things even in life's troubles. I believe you will find those things because at the centre of this book you will rediscover more of Jesus Christ through scripture, through life experiences and through the many rich quotations woven through the text. For some years Judy has tried to set Christ at the centre of her ministry, her preaching and teaching knowing that once Christ is set at the centre, everything else begins to fall into place.

Anyone reading this book on their own will gain much. But it is also a book written to inspire many conversations: between friends, between family members, in small groups, in those exploring vocation, among those on retreat together. It is a book people will want to give and share with others.

In the New Testament, waking from sleep is a picture of the resurrection: of rising with Christ to new life (Ephesians 5.14). I hope and pray that *A Kind of Sleepwalking* will bring new life and life in greater abundance to many people in all kinds of situations.

7

ACKNOWLEDGEMENTS

Writing my first book *Struggling to be Holy* felt at times like wringing water from a stone, but this book, as I am told second books often are, was even harder. As Steve Croft said when I rang him to say that after six years it was finally finished, 'It is nothing less than a miracle!' I am, of course, hoping that out of this struggle has emerged something which people might find helpful.

As before, I need to acknowledge the many people who have patiently supported me as I have tried to write. There are two people who particularly stand out. Firstly, I must thank my commissioning editor Virginia Hearn who has always kept faith with me and the book even when the going was hard and my energy and enthusiasm were flagging. I thank her from the bottom of my heart for her encouragement, her wise direction, her laughter and her care. Secondly, I started this book with the wise and loving accompaniment of my dear friend Ruth Etchells and felt it such a blow personally and in the process when Ruth died. I missed her so much and still do, but Ian Jagger kindly agreed to my request to accompany me and I have found him to be a deeply wise, godly, insightful and engaging companion. Deep thanks are also due to those who read various parts of the book and shared their own thoughts and perceptions, making what I was able to write much truer: John Lambert, Carol Simmons, Christine Evans, Alison Marshall, Helen Hornby, Rob Croft, Margaret Masson, David Slater, Stephen Cherry, Kate Bruce and Maeve

Sherlock. As always, I am deeply aware that this book reflects a shared wisdom which I have been privileged to express.

Authors and poets too numerous to mention here have been an inspiration in writing this book. I have written it in conversation between my own life and experience and that of many writers who have gone before. I would, however, particularly like to acknowledge the writings of Robert Ellsberg and Michael Mayne. It was reading Robert Ellsberg's book *The Saints' Guide to Happiness* which started me thinking about the issues in *A Kind of Sleepwalking* and I am aware of how much it has informed my thinking. It is a wonderful book, full of practical wisdom and insight. I have deeply loved all Michael Mayne's writings for many years and have read them and reread them often. They have become part of my deep heart and have taught me again and again especially about God's unconditional love and forgiveness and about joy. I also want to acknowledge all the people who have kindly listened to the material as it has been in formation: St Alban's Abbey during Holy Week where it was first let into the open, various retreats and quiet days, and St John's Neville's Cross, my thoughtful, questioning, accepting and generous home church who let me experiment with many ideas from the book during Lent last year.

I am very grateful to those people with whom I have a professional relationship as priest, spiritual director or counsellor, who have been generous enough to allow me to draw on their experiences in this book. I would also like to mention here my own spiritual director, Sue Morgan-Williams, who walks the way with me, supporting me, challenging me, keeping me safe and always trying to get me to understand God's deep love for me and all his wonderful creation. I am a very slow learner!

I have struggled to find space both physically and in the wonderfully complex kaleidoscope which is life and have been grateful several times for being rescued by St Anthony's Priory in Durham. They allowed me to escape from the daily demands of life and offered me a quiet, comfortable and beautiful space and one in which I was, most importantly, protected from interruptions.

9

As always, my husband John, my son James and daughter Beth and their spouses Louise and Anton have been alongside me in life encouraging me, putting up with me and teaching me many things. I want, however, to dedicate this book to my mother and father, Jean and Claude, who gave me life and taught me to love.

A KIND OF SLEEPWALKING

We all wake up in the morning in different ways. I often holiday with two friends I have known since childhood. They are impossibly early risers, having walked to the boulangerie for our bread and possibly swam and read a book before I emerge. It is amazing that the friendship has lasted so long. Those who know me well know that I hate mornings! I always struggle into the new day. When I wake up I often feel a bit anxious, vulnerable and easily overwhelmed, not yet really ready to face the world. My temptation is to rush into being busy and into my known routine, to distract myself from what I feel; either that or pull the duvet over my head, push the snooze button and wish the world would go away.

However, most days I do just try and get on with my life. I follow my familiar patterns and walk on well − beaten tracks, which I suspect is just about what most of us are capable of doing. But this mode of living is, I like to think, *a kind of sleepwalking*.

> To be awake is to be alive. I have not yet seen a man who was quite awake.[1]

This quote from Thoreau certainly rings bells with me; I am uncomfortably aware of my own unwillingness to wake up to life. Most of us, a lot of the time, sleepwalk through the landscape of our lives; the familiar and habitual are so reassuring that we are tempted to live there permanently, as though this is our ultimate reality. But in doing so we can lose sight of God's presence and of the truth of ourselves; the gap between who we have been created to be and the life we are living, unaware of our real purpose.

Fortunately I do not actually sleepwalk but I know some people who do. They tell me that they have no awareness of what they are doing until they jolt into being awake. Then they can find themselves in some pretty disorientating and scary places — one friend in a cupboard, another in a boiler room, and one hanging over a high-up banister in a Georgian farmhouse. They wonder, 'Where am I?' 'How did I get here and what am I doing here?' And it's scary! It can sometimes feel like that for us in life, as if we are waking up in a strange disorientating place, no longer seeing clearly where we are, who we are, how exactly life turned out to be like this. It usually takes some quite substantial issue to jolt us awake: it could be a death, a baby being born, a redundancy, falling in love, an illness, experiencing failure, or encountering real beauty.

The challenge then is to go deeper into ourselves and into God, but all sorts of doubts and anxieties can assail us:

'I'm scared of change.'

'I might get hurt.'

'What will others think of me?'

'I might lose control.'

'Do I really add up to anything worthwhile?'

'Have I been wasting my time and effort chasing after things I am not sure matter any more?'

'I am not the person I thought I was or thought I could be.'

All life's experiences have the potential to be life-giving, even, and maybe especially, those which hurt and scare us. This book is an attempt to help us to hold on to some of these moments of truth and awakening; to chew them over and be taught by them. It tries to encourage us to give them their chance to speak to us and sometimes for us; to begin to see the flimsiness of the way the world lives its life compared to the reality of what God's way of life has to offer.

We need to begin to listen to our lives, to let them share their mysteries; life can teach us all we yearn to know, any life can do this if we are open to it. Moments which wake us up from our sleepwalking are like unopened gifts on the journey. It is in and through our awakened attention to the daily, ordinary events and the created world that what is hidden can be sought and hopefully found. We need to learn to pay attention if we are not to miss the moment. We are invited to accept and work on the raw material which we are offered in our own unique lives to deal with the stuff of our daily experiences which provides us with glimpses of God's reality.

I believe that all of us in our lives experience moments of truth and of revelation, moments of being woken up. In our grasp is the realisation that there is something lacking and that we are in the presence of something which is beyond and other than ourselves, which raises acute questions about how we are living our lives. Such moments may be forced by the hard things of life: grief, loss, suffering, growing older, but they may also arise when listening to Mozart, watching children play, looking at the stars, sitting by a waterfall, gazing into the eyes of the one we love, or in worship.

These moments can take us, however briefly, out of our normal existence and wake us up to the deeper meanings and issues of life. I believe that we are brought into closer, clearer, less cluttered contact with God's truth. God's spirit promises to bring us into the truth by stripping away the barriers and insulation which separate us from living contact with reality: the reality of God; the reality of God's world and the reality of our true selves. Thomas Merton wrote that 'the gate of heaven is everywhere'.[2] If that is true, daily life, anyone's daily life, can become the road to heaven, however improbable that might seem at times.

A seeker asked a monk, 'Where should I look for spiritual enlightenment?'
The monk said, 'Here'.
The seeker said, 'When will it happen?'
'It's happening right now,' said the monk.
'Then why don't I experience it?'
'Because you don't look.'
'So what should I look for?' asked the seeker.
'Nothing,' said the monk. 'Just look.'
'At what?'

'Anything your eyes light upon.'

The seeker was getting perplexed. 'Must I look in a special way?' he asked.

'No,' said the monk, 'the ordinary way will be fine.'

'But don't I always look the ordinary way?'

'No, you don't.'

'Why ever not?' demanded the seeker.

'Because to look you must be here,' said the monk, 'and you're mostly somewhere else.'[3]

The spiritual journey starts with our being present to our own lives and attending to God who is always present. This story tells us that we don't normally need to look far from our ordinary, everyday lives to find what we are seeking.

'I find my bearings when I become lost.'[4]

My husband John likes to drive, but like many men he will never, on principle, ask the way. I know with a sinking heart that we are lost ages before he does. He remains confident that our destination is 'just around the corner' or that we are 'nearly there'. Finally the truth dawns on John that *we are lost*. (I have to say that the invention of the satnav has helped our marriage considerably!)

In life the search starts from noticing that we are lost, but this can take years for us to realise. Whenever the moment of awakening happens we discover that all we had previously understood about life and living just does not seem to work so well or make so much sense any more. As we are jolted awake from our sleepwalking we discover that our life's journey has run into the sand.

Although this can feel a terrible place to be, it is potentially an improvement, a huge step forward. However, the temptation is to run for cover, to get back on the old track, to return to the known, the safe, the tried and tested. So we re-immerse ourselves in busy and demanding work schedules, distracting ourselves with material things, with leisure or with people. None of these are bad in themselves, but if they distract us from dealing with the issues which are arising then we do not find our bearings. We need to sit with the reality to which we are being awoken, to face the truth of our situation and the emptiness and confusion within.

My mum was doing a jigsaw. She loves to do jigsaws in the cold, dark winter's evenings. This particular jigsaw was a nightmare, full of blue sea and almost identical blue sky. Mum gamely ploughed on assessing each piece and putting it in place. She seemed to be doing well until she was brought to a halt; nothing more would fit. The blank in the middle simply refused to be filled however hard Mum tried. Finally she realised, having been halted, that she had confused some of the sea pieces with some of the sky pieces. Things were not as they seemed to be. She reassessed the situation and decided that there was nothing for it but to start to break up what she had so painstakingly built up. She started again, wiser this time about the subtly different hues of sky and sea.

I tell this story because it offers a good illustration of life. We do the best we can and believe that we are doing okay and making progress, then something happens and we find ourselves faced with the reality that we are stuck: that things don't make sense, that we are going to have to stop and re-evaluate, that we may need to change and unpick and redo some of what we have done and what we are. It can feel like having to start again and this can be very painful.

> Midway this way of life we are bound upon
> I woke to find myself in a dark wood
> Where the road was wholly lost and gone.[5]

In such moments of re-evaluation we are offered the opportunity to see things differently, but to negotiate this new territory we need to discover new signposts. Our spiritual life is always in need of transformation but it is only ever possible when we wake up and come to terms with what we see; then we start to be able to discern God's reality and God's way. Life, after all, is often a struggle: none of us enjoys success without some failure, no one lives a pain-free life, and we all feel anxious and vulnerable at times, as well as feeling on top of the world at others. Good times and bad times, all times which shake us awake can begin to integrate us into the real life of God. They can help us start to get a different handle on life, beyond the immediate and the obvious, a different kind of reality not as we imagine it but as it really is.

> There is another world, but it is in this one.[6]

Jesus' words and behaviour always confront us with this other way of reality: God's way. As an example let us consider the story in Luke 7[7] about Simon the Pharisee, a professional religious person, and, the person my Bible calls 'the sinful woman'. Simon had invited Jesus to have dinner with him; we don't know why. Perhaps he liked collecting interesting people or was an admirer or sympathiser, but none of this seems likely as he treated Jesus with such discourtesy. Perhaps he wanted this rather startling young rabbi as a curiosity to enliven his dinner table. Whatever the reason, it soon became clear that Jesus was on trial. He was there to be observed and weighed up, to see if the rumours about him being a prophet were true.

What was immediately apparent was Simon's lack of even the most basic hospitality. He failed to give Jesus any water for his feet or to offer a kiss of welcome. His omissions are outrageously rude and the story encourages us to set this against the outrageous adoration of the woman. I do so wish we knew her name! Let's try and visualise the scene. She is probably a prostitute. We need to recall how prostitutes look, how they dress: no sophistication and much raw sexiness ... the make-up, the high heels. Obviously this woman would not actually look like this but you get the flavour. When she arrived it would have caused quite a stir, people would not have known where to look. She appeared and started her extraordinary ministrations. You can well imagine eyes popping out, bated breath and, from Simon at least, immediate judgement. If Jesus was prepared to receive this from her then he was definitely not the man people were saying he was. Simon could not begin to appreciate God's generous love even when it was sitting at his table!

Nothing could be in sharper contrast with this than the passionate, generous offering of this woman. She offered the best that she had in a little phial of concentrated perfume which was very costly. She wept in gratitude for the forgiveness of her sins and wiped away her tears from Jesus' feet with her hair — a very intimate act and quite outrageous in a culture where letting your hair down in public was an indecent thing to do. Then she kissed his feet; not just one chaste kiss — as Jesus said to Simon, 'She has never stopped kissing my feet since I got here.'

This picture is supposed to stop us in our tracks, to shock us, *to wake us up*. If this woman's actions are okay, even more, if they are good and to be commended by Jesus, how far away from this are we? Are we nearer in heart and action to Simon or to this woman? As with other encounters in the Gospels, we are apparently to understand that a sinful prostitute is nearer to God than the righteous Pharisee; the dissolute prodigal son nearer to God than the dutiful older son, and the blind beggar Bartimaeus richer than the rich, young ruler. As we see time and time again Jesus turns our expectations upside down; social conventions are thrown out of the window. Human beings do not appear as society sees them but as God sees them according to his reality, and most of us, like Simon, are left standing! Wherever Jesus is, God's reality is staring us in the face. It is this reality we need to try

and see beyond our sleepwalking and, if we can, wake
up to it.

When we love, when we tell ourselves we do,
we are pining for first love, somewhen,
before we thought of wanting it. When we rearrange
the rooms we end up living in, we are looking
for first light, the arrangement of light,
that time, before we knew to call it light.

Or talk of music, when we say
we cannot talk of it, but play again
C major, A flat minor, we are straining
for first sound, what we heard once,
then, in lost chords, wordless languages.

What country do we come from? This one?
The one where the sun burns
when we have night? The one
the moon chills; elsewhere, possible?

Why is our love imperfect,
music only echo of itself,
the light wrong?

We scratch in dust with sticks,
dying of homesickness
for when, where, what. [8]

Carol Ann Duffy

FOR DISCUSSION

1. Does the idea of 'sleepwalking' through life ring any bells with you? Can you give some examples?

2. Can you remember a time when you were jolted awake from 'sleepwalking'? What caused this to happen?

3. How do you react to the list on p.12 of the reasons why we often choose not to go deeper into ourselves and into God?

4. Does the story about the seeker and the monk on p.14 make any sense to you? In what ways? Do you believe that life, any life, can teach us what we need to know, that, as Thomas Merton says, 'the gate of heaven is everywhere?'.

5. Can you think of times in your own life when you have 'woken up' to the fact that you have lost your way?

6. How do you respond to the story about the author's mother and her jigsaw (p.16)?

7. Why do you think we are often tempted when 'woken up' to run for cover, to return to the known, the safe, the tried and tested?

8. Does Paul Eluard's quotation 'There is another world, but it is in this one?' make any sense to you?

9. How do you respond to the concept of 'homesickness' in Carol Ann Duffy's poem on p.20?

BIBLE PASSAGE FOR
REFLECTION: LUKE 7:36-50

1. How did Simon treat Jesus and why do you think he did this?
2. Compare Simon's actions with those of 'the woman'. What do you think was motivating her?
3. What on earth would we have made of such an event if it had happened in our church or our home?
4. What are the profound issues of judgement and forgiveness in this story?
5. Are you nearer in heart and action to 'the woman' or to Simon? Why?
6. What do you understand God's reality to be like as illustrated in this story?

CLOSING PRAYER

Lord, teach me to seek you,
And reveal yourself to me as I look for you.
For I cannot seek you unless first you teach me,
Nor find you unless first you reveal yourself to me.

St Ambrose 340-97

2

WAKING UP TO SUFFERING

The day was perfect; the sort of summer's day which brings back the long carefree days of childhood. The sky was blue, the sunshine warm, and the breeze gentle upon my face as I drove along, window wide open, among golden wheat fields full of bird song. Bliss! Well, not quite bliss, not even near in fact, because the purpose of the trip through this perfect landscape was to bury a man in his early forties. He was a wonderful person who had struggled long and hard with cancer, and was leaving behind a grieving wife, four distraught teenage children and bemused parents. What sort of world is this exactly?

It is the world we know. A world shot through with matchless beauty yet witness at the same time to intolerable pain and suffering. George Fox, the first Quaker, described it accurately as 'an ocean of darkness and death, as well as an infinite ocean of light and love'.[1] This is how it is, like it or not; this bemusing contradiction in which we are invited to make sense of our lives. The challenge then is to be faithful to both without compromising the truth.

Mostly we simply deal with this by evading the

issue. In our affluent world that is quite easy although recent economic developments have made it more of a challenge. Nonetheless, we are lucky that for most of us, most of the time we are not living in the context described in the Book of Common Prayer as 'in the midst of life is death'. It is there of course, but usually far off and very well managed to inconvenience us and impinge on our reality as little as possible. We have the wherewithal to keep suffering at bay in ways which the developing world can only dream of. So when suffering comes along it is seen as an aberration, an accident which should not happen, and when it does rear its ugly head we naturally, and quite rightly, go to great lengths to ensure that it won't happen again: from huge sums of money spent on medical research to compulsory seatbelts on coaches and massive sea defences, to name some examples. All are attempts to keep suffering at bay.

But the hard truth is that suffering is an integral part of the world as we know it. Suffering is a fact of life. We are, whether we like it or not, creatures who suffer. The truth is that the thread of suffering runs so deeply through the fabric of our existence that were it pulled free the remnant would unravel beyond recognition.[2] Just think about it for a moment. Think about your own life: the various sufferings caused by failure or disappointment, suffering caused by illness of body or mind, of hurts and damage caused by anger and relationships. Even if we could avoid serious suffering ourselves then waiting in the wings for us are the diminishments and losses of old age and the fact that others whom we love will suffer: our parents, our children, our friends, and we will feel deep anguish on their behalf. The truth is that we are schooled in suffering; it is at the very core of our being.

However, in our culture of affluence and entitlement we are encouraged to believe and behave as if suffering is somehow extrinsic to human life, an aberration, an accident which somehow befalls others and not us. And yet deep down we all know, don't we, that this is not our reality, and suppressing this truth is at least one reason for the depression which is endemic in our society. It takes a huge amount of energy to evade the truth of suffering all the time and such an evasion will finally, inevitably, fail us.

When suffering comes its arrival stops everything dead:

'You're fired!'

'You only have three months to live.'

'Your child has cystic fibrosis.'

'I do not want to stay married to you.'

Suffering arrives, shattering and unravelling our world: jolting us awake. This is an awful, painful place, yet somehow we need to be able to recognise that it is at these moments when we can in fact move forward, but it is difficult because in pain we struggle to find the capacity to deal with what is happening.

So what is to be done? We are perhaps called to try to live life with our eyes open to all the contradictions and suffering. We are invited not to collude with the many distraction techniques of the world. We see clearly in Jesus' life, as Henri Nouwen points out, that 'Real joy and peace can never be reached by bypassing suffering and death but only by going right through them.'[3] Jesus, in other words, takes up his cross because there is no other way. So how do we learn to deal more creatively with suffering?

At one level it just happens to us all. When suffering grips us it takes over and nothing else really seems to matter. It changes our priorities and transforms our world. I sometimes imagine it like a prism. That we live our lives looking through a prism which is slightly out of focus and that when we suffer it is as if the prism shifts bringing everything into sharp focus making priorities clear. Several times when I was faced with what could have been life-shattering medical issues all confusion fell away. For me the simple priority of people was absolutely evident and the neglect of them totally unjustifiable:

Suddenly when you hear a friend died young, you stop worrying about the new kitchen.

When you are called back for more tests, the status in which you are held seems less pressing.

When your child is being bullied, that much-sought-after promotion seems less important.

When your child dies, suddenly all the reasons why you did not spend more time with them make no sense any more.

So suffering can expose our vanities and our hollowness and can challenge our assumptions about life. The turn of the prism makes things crystal clear for the first time; we find we are awake. Suffering, if it strips away our illusions and makes us see more clearly, can be both a merciful friend and a profound spiritual guide. It can bring us face to face with ourselves.

The fire of suffering cleanses completely the falsities to which our longing has attached itself. This liberates us from the emptiness of false belonging and allows us to belong in a real and truthful way in our lives again. Truth is difficult to reach and endure; but it is always the doorway to new freedom and life.[4]

Suffering knocks us off our tracks, but it can be exactly in this place that we can grow. We can no longer help ourselves and so begin to face the truth of our helplessness. 'If you see a young man ascending to heaven by his own will pull him down again!' said the Desert Fathers.[5] Suffering pulls us down and slows us down, diminishing and messing up our lives. We hate it! But it does bring the gift of limiting our life, of paring it back to essentials, to a place where we can learn things that are not often possible in our busy lives. A story from the Egyptian monks of the fourth century illustrates this well:

A young newcomer to the monastery asks what he should do to grow in holiness. He is told to sit in his cell, to pray at dawn and to pray at dusk. This seems insufficiently challenging, so he seeks advice from a second monk who tells him to pray only once and apart from that keep to his cell. Now thoroughly fed up he seeks the advice of a third elder: 'Sit in your cell', he is told, 'and your cell will teach you everything!'[6]

Often we like him, will do almost anything to evade sitting with ourselves quietly. We want to steer clear of being confronted with all the things which we routinely try to avoid. Our frenetic world acts as an excellent distraction from the things which really matter and we are at risk of living in almost permanent denial. It often takes some form of suffering to shake us awake and to help us to grow as people. In the words of the early church fathers, 'As wax cannot take the imprint of a seal unless it is warmed or softened thoroughly, so a person cannot receive the seal of God's holiness unless he is tested by suffering.'[7]

We see this in the lives of many of the great saints. St Francis of Assisi was a young man who, one of his many biographers claims, 'squandered and wasted his life miserably', a man who 'outdid his contemporaries in vanities, pomp and vainglory'. A nice young lad then! The turning point came for Francis through the twin sufferings of war and a prolonged illness. Again this biographer tells us that these events 'gave him time to think of things other than he was used to thinking upon and he began to hold in contempt the person he had been and the things he had admired and loved'. There were, of course, other steps which led Francis into his new life, but what is important for us to note is how his suffering woke him up and offered him a completely different way of seeing, which started to teach him how to be truly alive.[8]

We all have muscles which we don't use much – me, personally, far too many! Similarly we all have so many aspects of our humanity which lie dormant, half used – living our life in a kind of sleepwalking. We need something to wake us up, some experience which will shake us into life. Of course, that can be a delightful experience — like falling in love, for example, or becoming a parent — but often, while we wouldn't seek or choose it, it is suffering of some sort. Leon Bloy, the French novelist, wrote: 'In our poor hearts we have places which do not yet exist and into them enters suffering in order to bring life.'[9]

We also instinctively know when others have suffered and been transformed by their suffering rather than letting it destroy them. These are the people we often turn to for help, recognising the compassion, empathy and understanding which suffering has wrought in them.

I had tried many times to write this reflection on suffering, often writing from a position of relative competence and confidence, and I have failed. I am now actually writing this during a time of great pain for my family and an experience of great powerless in the face of injustice for me. I am struggling with this more than I can say, but it has woken me up in a way which has allowed me to express what I feel is true about this subject.

What do we learn then? Well, certainly we learn about priorities. Suffering turns our priorities on their heads. We also definitely learn something crucial about living in the present moment, but perhaps above all we learn that we are not in control. Despite all our best efforts to protect ourselves and our families we are in fact vulnerable. But is this learning worth the price? Is it worth the suffering? Well, personally, having experienced some suffering, I would not sign up for it! I would not voluntarily 'take up my cross', and this makes me even more amazed and grateful at what Christ has done for me.

A few years ago I had surgery on my sinuses. When I came out of the anaesthetic I could hardly breathe through my nose or my mouth and I had the experience of feeling I was suffocating. I panicked and it was absolutely terrifying. This feeling was, of course, very short lived because as my panic subsided I realised that I could in fact breathe through my mouth, though that was difficult because I had not had anything to drink for many, many hours. Soon after this short but intense experience of real physical and mental suffering I was invited to speak in a service in Durham Cathedral in Holy Week. I found myself absolutely overwhelmed that Christ was prepared to suffer for me; it now had a whole new meaning. I knew that I would never have been willing to voluntarily suffer in this way. I felt humbled, profoundly moved and deeply grateful.

So we wouldn't sign up for it, but as it happens suffering seeks us out anyway. It does not of course necessarily make us nicer or holier. It can lead to bitterness, anger, resentment, self-pity or despair. Suffering is not of itself good, but Christians believe that God is good and that he can take our suffering and make it productive and transformative. It is our response and our attitude which is crucial.

I am reminded of the two thieves on the cross with Jesus. For each the physical circumstances of their suffering were similar but their inner response was in marked contrast to each other. One spent his dying moments on spiteful taunts, and the other addressed Jesus with trust, saying 'Lord, remember me in your kingdom'. For one, his physical suffering was compounded by resentment and bitterness, whereas the other was able in some way to transcend his circumstances and touch eternity. 'This day,' says Jesus 'you shall be with me in eternity.'[10]

It is essential that we understand that God does not will suffering, but the challenge for us is how to seek God's presence in every circumstance. The challenge is also how to have a realistic understanding of how God can and does engage with suffering. Over the years I have encountered so many people who have abandoned faith in God because of God's failure in their eyes to rescue them or others from suffering; for God's failure to fix things. In this present trouble for my family, when I was moaning about how little help God was being, a dear friend challenged me by saying, 'So, Judy, this God who is not engaged and helping ... does she have a pink fluffy dress and a magic wand in her hand?' I must say, apart from making me laugh, the thought stopped me in my tracks.

I was reminded of the account of Jesus calming the storm in Luke 8[11] in which there are many valuable lessons. I used this story on a retreat and invited people to imagine themselves into the story. How would you behave in this situation?

Maybe you would either not know or in your panic forget that Jesus was on board the boat.

Maybe you would be too frightened to wake him up, not wanting to bother him.

Maybe you would straight away rush panicking to him (that's more my style!).

Maybe you would just need to know he was near and then be able to carry on and feel okay.

Whatever the disciples' response, the storm *was* allowed to occur and Jesus' presence in the boat did not prevent it happening. The storm was allowed to happen, Luke tells us, until they were in real danger. I imagine this bunch of seasoned fishermen were fine to begin with, confident in their skills and knowledge of the lake. Perhaps they were gradually pushed out of their comfort zone until they finally had to wake Jesus. You can imagine the scene on the boat: to begin with the disciples were probably working well together, having a bit of a joke, then maybe recriminations start to grow as they become more afraid:

'I told you the weather looked bad.'

'I never thought we should have gone out today.'

Gradually the danger increased, as did the feeling of fear and of being out of control. When Jesus is finally awoken (I don't suppose as a carpenter he would be your first thought in this crisis) it always seems that the miracle is done rather unwillingly. The impression is irresistible that the better way would have been for the disciples to have passed through the storm confidently, trustingly and that the miracle was worked as a concession to their weakness. 'Why are you fearful? How is it you have no faith?' After all, Jesus was in the boat with them, do they still not understand who he is?

Storms are never welcome. We much prefer peace, calm and control but we learn from this episode that they are allowed to happen and happen to the point where we feel that we cannot cope at all, where we are powerless and have lost hope. We also see that Jesus was in the storm with them but he let the storm take its course. The disciples, knowing he was there (or had they forgotten?), were unable to trust him in such difficult circumstances.

Sometimes God does seem to remove the storm, but usually we find that we have to endure it. I am reminded of the disciple Peter who thought that he had got the hang of things after his uncomfortable encounter with Jesus when he resisted having his feet washed.[12] He found instead that he had not really learned anything until the storm of his denial.[13] Jesus knew it would come and knew that it must come. Jesus understood that Peter needed to crash down far enough to be empty and desperate enough for the love of God; to go down enough to know his own truth. Storms expose us. They change our landscape. I was living in a 60-acre oak wood during the hurricane of 1987. I knew the wood like the back of my hand but after the hurricane I went for a walk and got lost, the storm had so profoundly altered the landscape. What is always fascinating to me is that Jesus does not pray that the storm won't come for Peter, presumably because he knows how desperately Peter needs the transformation it will bring. Instead Jesus tells Peter that he has prayed, 'That his faith won't fail' when the storm comes and also that when he has recovered and turned back he will be able to use what he has learned to strengthen his brothers.[14]

We need to learn to see our lives illuminated by the

story of Christ. Not just in the wonderful moments but in the misunderstandings, the pain of rejection, the betrayal and abandonment of friends, the loneliness, the anxiety, the powerlessness, the fear of suffering and suffering itself, the humiliation and terrible physical and mental pain. We have limited control over the circumstances of our lives and that is the hard truth. What we do have, though, is the choice in every circumstance of suffering to shape our attitude to it; to hand it over to God or to withhold it from him. To trust him with it or to give up hope.

Sheila Cassidy,[15] an English doctor working in Chile during the military coup, was arrested and tortured for treating a wounded revolutionary. Her first instinct was to scream out to God for help, but then she says that a curious idea came to her, that she would hold out her hands in offering. In her book *Audacity to Believe* she writes, 'In my powerlessness, suffering and captivity there remained to me one freedom: I could abandon myself into the hands of God.' When we suffer we feel terribly out of control and this can only be transformed by giving it to God. Of course, this prayer did not bring an instant change in her attitude but gradually helped her to find the necessary courage and strength to deal with her horrendous circumstances, to enable her to take up her cross rather than to be crushed by it.

The experience of being a political prisoner is exceptional but later, as a doctor in a hospice, Sheila Cassidy found that her experience in Chile had given her some common ground with her terminally ill patients. She discovered that insights drawn from her own encounter with suffering might apply to anyone in desperate circumstances, circumstances which they are powerless to alter: 'In suffering we can spend our energy in bitterness and despair battering our wings against the cage or we can come alongside God in prayer and take up our cross.'

We need to learn to live by the assurance that there is meaning and a truth at the heart of life which suffering is ultimately powerless to destroy. I am reminded here of Job in the Old Testament. He refused to curse God despite all his extreme suffering and accepted that to completely understand suffering was impossible: 'Surely I spoke of things I did not understand, things too wonderful for me to know.'[16] Suffering is not good, but God is good, and as the apostle Paul wrote, 'neither death, nor life, nor height, nor depth can deprive us of access to that good if we truly desire it'.[17] Jesus takes up his cross because there is no other way for this world. As Henri Nouwen reminds us, 'Real joy and peace can never be reached by bypassing suffering and death but only by going right through.'

High above in the Octagon at Ely Cathedral (itself a picture of resurrection after disaster as it replaced a tower that suddenly collapsed in a heap of rubble in 1322) is the image of the risen, ascended Christ surrounded by angels. His right hand is raised in blessing and his left hand is pulling away his clothing to reveal the still raw, deep red wound in his side. This risen Christ is not as he was before the crucifixion. He is not some perfect Christ without blemish untouched by his suffering. He is not restored to exactly how he was before. He has changed. Pain and suffering have changed him and he still has the wounds. He is not risen pristine, he is risen wounded and I guess that is where many of our lives are as well. We are challenged neither to be trapped forever by the pain of our suffering as if there were no resurrection nor to behave as if nothing has happened. We need to learn to hold together those things which seem in sharp contradiction: pain and hope, anger and love, tears and laughter; to face the grim reality of our circumstances of suffering without losing sight of eternity; to be restored into the image of his glory; the image of our 'risen, wounded' Lord.[18]

Ah my deare, angry Lord,
Since thou dost love yet strike;
Cast down yet help afford;
Sure I will do the like.

I will complain, yet praise;
I will bewail, approve;
And all my sour-sweet days
I will lament and love.[19]

FOR DISCUSSION

1. Can you share some examples of suffering which have either affected you personally or affected others you know?

2. 'Suffering is a fact of life.' How do you respond to this statement?

3. When suffering comes, in what ways does it affect our lives? Do you find the 'prism' illustration (p.26) used by the author to be true to life or not?

4. Henri Nouwen wrote: 'Real joy and peace can never be reached by bypassing suffering and death but only by going right through them.' How does this view sit in a world which pursues happiness so vigorously?

5. 'Suffering strips away illusions and makes us see more clearly' (p.28). Do you agree with this statement? Can you give some examples?

6. Read the story on p.29 about the monk in his cell. Do you agree with the point it is making? Why do you think we are so keen to steer clear of being confronted with ourselves and our lives?

7. In her book *Audacity to Believe*, Sheila Cassidy writes that: 'In suffering we can spend our energy in

bitterness and despair battering our wings against the cage or we can come alongside God in prayer and take up our cross.' How do you respond to this idea?

8. Do you agree that suffering teaches us that we are not in control? Have you any experiences of feeling this?

9. Discuss the idea that God does not will suffering but that we need to seek God's presence in it? Does this ring true to you?

10. Do you find the idea of 'risen wounded' rather than 'risen pristine' speaks to your life (p.38)? Can you think of ways in which you still carry the wounds of previous suffering?

BIBLE PASSAGE FOR
REFLECTION: LUKE 8:22-25

1. The author invites you to imagine yourself in the storm? How do you think you would have reacted (p.33)?

2. Despite the fact that Jesus was in the boat, this storm was allowed to happen, to happen until those on board were in real danger. How does this help you reflect upon such 'storms' in your own life?

3. Jesus, having calmed the storm, says to the disciples, 'Why are you fearful? How is it you have no faith?' In what way does this challenge us when we are visited by suffering?

4. Storms expose us and change our landscape (p.35). Do you have any examples of this from your own experience?

5. Jesus allowed Peter to fail and to suffer so that he could receive the transformation he so desperately needed. He prays for Peter that when the storm comes 'his faith won't fail'. What do you think this might mean in our own lives?

CLOSING PRAYER

O God,
Early in the morning I cry unto you.
Help me to pray
And to think only of you.
I cannot pray alone.
In me there is darkness
But with you there is light.
I am lonely but you do not leave me.
I am feeble in heart but you do not leave me.
I am restless but with you there is peace.
In me there is bitterness, but with you there is
    patience.
Your ways are past understanding, but
You know the way for me.

Dietrich Bonhoeffer in Angela Ashwin (ed.),
The Book of a Thousand Prayers
(Marshall Pickering, 1996), p.83

3

WAKING UP TO WONDER

It had been an average day. Well, if I'm honest it had been a less than average day because I had to visit the dentist. I absolutely loathe going to the dentist, although Graeme my dentist is himself charming. I had been mercifully and unexpectedly released with no treatment and having some time to spare decided to walk in the nearby churchyard.

Some days, most days, we simply do what has to be done; days furnished with all the ordinary trappings of life. Then sometimes, not often and quite unexpectedly, there are days and bits of days which are of quite another order altogether. Happiness descends out of nowhere. Ordinary things seem extraordinary. Life is unexceptional and then all of a sudden it is not; it becomes full of wonder. As I walked I became acutely aware of the smell of the earth, the beauty of the snowdrops, the birds singing, and as I followed the path out of the trees I was stunned by the view of Durham Cathedral: the sandstone glowing with golden sunlight. I stopped and stared, knowing it would be like this for a very short time. At one moment life was quite unexceptional and then all of a sudden it was not: it became a marvel and I was filled with wonder. I was held by the beauty of it. It was speaking to me.

On retreats I sometimes invite people to share such experiences and I discover that such moments of awareness occur to many people. One marvellous example is shared in J. V. Taylor's book *A Matter of Life and Death*.

I think perhaps I was six. I was taken to the park in the evening to enjoy a firework display. It was summer. There was a crowd of people by the lake … Against the darkening sky, before the fireworks were set alight, I remember seeing these trees, poplar trees they were, three of them. It is very difficult to say exactly what happened because the order of the experience is of its own kind. There was a breeze and the leaves of the poplars vibrated, rustled. I believe I said to myself, 'How beautiful, how wonderful those trees are.' I think there was awe and wonder, and I remember luminousness – that's a grown up word of course – the marvellous beauty, the haunting oppressive power of those trees with the artificiality of the surroundings, the people, and the fireworks and so on. Oddly, I kind of knew that this was something extraordinary at the moment it occurred. It was as simple as that, just seeing these trees, but it was the event of my childhood … I knew then it was going to last. And so it has … What happened was telling me something. But what was it telling? The fact of divinity, that it was good? … not so much in the moral sense, but that it was beautiful, yes, sacred.[1]

44

Children know all about wonder and so did we once, but we unlearn it as adults. To a child the world is filled with wonder; just try doing a very short walk with a three-year-old delighting in bits of this and that. A friend told me recently of taking her three-year-old grandson Ben to soft play at the leisure centre. They were driving down to the banks of the River Tyne, terraced houses running down to the river in long, uniform rows: a *Billy Elliot* scene! Suddenly from the back seat a small voice piped up, 'Isn't this beautiful, Granny and Grandpa!' My friend and her husband glanced at each other – no offence to the inhabitants of Newburn, but beautiful probably would not be the first adjective that came to mind. Ben, however, was seeing things for the first time and beauty was what he saw!

Although we are not as gifted as children at seeing the wonder, most of us know something of this. If you ask people they will give you examples: of being moved by nature, by children, by art, by poetry, by their gardens, by rivers, by the sea, by music. These are moments which are hard to explain but they are when the ordinary speaks of the extraordinary: when we are awoken from our sleepwalking to another reality and look around with utter bewilderment and delight at what we see. The particular object does not really matter. The essential element is that all these experiences wake us up, connect us to a different view of the world and fill us with life and love. They are often reported with similar characteristics, e.g. we struggle to find the right language to speak of them sensing they are somehow a different order of knowing; they are fleeting; time seems to be suspended and we experience a harmony with the whole of creation. All agree that these experiences are life affirming and good and we don't ever forget them. The poet Edwin Muir sums up this last point beautifully in his poem, 'The Labyrinth':

That was the real world: I have touched it once,
And now shall know it always.[2]

Waking up involves beginning to notice that the world is calling to us, that living alongside us, only hidden by the thinnest of veils, is the reality we seek , the reality which we need to encounter. However, with our distracted busyness, the simple task of being present can defeat us. The challenge is given well by Mary Oliver:

My work is loving the world.
Here the sunflowers, there the hummingbird—
     equal seekers of sweetness.
Here the quickening yeast; there the blue plums.
Here the clam deep in the speckled sand.

Are my boots old? Is my coat torn?
Am I no longer young and still not half perfect? Let
     me keep my mind on what matters,
which is my work,

which is mostly standing still and learning to be
     astonished.
The phoebe, the delphinium.
The sheep in the pasture, and the pasture.

which is mostly rejoicing, since all the ingredients
    are here.

which is gratitude, to be given a mind and a heart
    and these body-clothes,
a mouth with which to give shouts of joy
    to the moth and the wren, to the sleepy dug-up
    clam,
telling them all, over and over, how it is
    that we live forever.[3]

The world has been created by God as the place where we can exercise all our human powers of creativity, imagination and interpretation. As Michael Mayne says in his inspiring book *This Sunrise of Wonder*: 'Our role in the world which is given to us is to wonder at it, to explore it and to restore to it and to our own lives true meaning.'[4] The whole created order and our response of wonder to it is given so that we can get in touch with reality, God's reality, the true meaning of our lives.

I have always thought it odd why certain things do move us so profoundly. We have been thinking about the natural world. As I am writing I am looking out of my window on to a blue sky full of towering cumulus clouds. They are beautiful and astonishing and yet they are functional, there to recycle water in our system. I often wonder why we perceive these as beautiful. As my friends and family know I am never happier than when walking or sitting by a river. Whether it is my beloved River Itchen in Hampshire, the one with which I grew up – a chalk stream, sparkling clear water, bright green weed, gravel bottomed and full of trout – or the wilder, more rocky, tumbling Pennine rivers, peat brown, which I have come to love while living in Durham, I am content. Either way, I find them beautiful but in fact they are again functional; a way of transporting water which falls on the land to the sea. As Graham Swift observes: 'Why should there be certain things in this random universe which cry out to us with their loveliness?'[5] It is strange how matter is capable of being the bearer of the spiritual, that things have the power to speak beyond themselves and to move us, that they point beyond themselves to God. They make us think that there must be something more, something beyond the everyday sights and sounds.

The natural world is not the only medium for wonder. It is also a mystery why certain combinations of words are poetry and certain combinations of musical notes are a symphony and certain colours on a canvas are a painting, and a bigger mystery that these things can strike at our feelings and understandings with such intensity. I love poetry and paintings; there is no more shelf space or wall space in our house! A good painting helps us to interpret and experience a particular scene, person or object. It helps us to see reality differently, intensifying our awareness and leading us to wonder. It should stop us in our tracks; wake us up. All good art, music, poetry and drama cause us to question how things are, how they *really* are. We are surprised away from the obvious and known and challenged to see things differently. We seem to have forgotten who and what we are and these prompts help us to remember; they are all windows into deeper reality and into our hearts. It always amuses me that the first play I ever went to was Becket's *Waiting for Godot* ... quite an introduction to the theatre for a fifteen-year-old! I had no real idea what it was about, but I was riveted. It made me think; I can honestly say it woke me up. You will be glad to know that I have seen many more hopeful and enjoyable plays since.

Although always surrounded by wonder, we are more open at some times than others to receive it. An obvious trigger could be when we are told we may not have much longer to live, or when we feel in danger that might be the case. The day before I went to have an operation I took my two, then young, children to a local park which edges onto beautiful open countryside where a river cuts around a steep hillside. That day, I experienced everything with a particular clarity and sharpness wondering if I would ever be there again to experience the trickling sound of the river, the bright yellow gorse bushes, the bird song, the laughter of my children. That was many years ago now but I still walk my dog Gracie there occasionally and I sometimes experience the intense wonder of that day reminding me of how good it is to be alive and well.

Certainly imminent death focuses attention: quickly forcing us to discern what is essential and what is irrelevant and to see the world differently. When the playwright Dennis Potter was facing death from terminal cancer he spoke of experiencing life with a fresh intensity. He said in a television interview with Melvyn Bragg that:

The only thing you know for sure is the present

tense; and that nowness becomes so vivid that, almost in a perverse sort of way, I'm almost serene. You know I can celebrate life. Below my window in Ross ... at this season, the blossom is out in full now ... it's white, and looking at it, instead of saying 'Oh that's nice blossom'... last week looking at it through the window while writing, I see it is the whitest, frothiest, blossomest blossom that there ever could be and I can see it ... The nowness of everything is absolutely wondrous, and if people could see that.[6]

How *could* we have never noticed before? J. V. Taylor records this wonderful prayer written by a young man a few days after the outbreak of the First World War:

To have given me self-consciousness for an hour in a world so breathless with beauty would have been enough. But thou hast preserved it within me for twenty years now and more, thou hast crowned it with the joy of this summer of summers. And so, come what may, whether life or death, and if death, whether bliss unimaginable or nothing, I thank thee and bless thy name.[7]

A very wide awake young man who sadly not long after he wrote this was killed in the trenches.

As we face up to the loss of the sights and sounds of the world it wonderfully concentrates the mind and it sharpens up our experience of it and our longing. Death and illness force us to just be, but this is the journey of our life; learning to live receptively in the present. If we believe in a sacramental world we believe that God inhabits his creation and can be discovered in it. As the poet Emily Dickinson wrote:

The only news I know,
Is bulletins all day
From immortality.[8]

The fact that any one of us lives is a miracle and the probability of our particular existence is billions to one. One of my absolutely prized possessions is an old, faded, red Rizla cigarette paper box. It is filled with shrapnel, heavy and jagged, that was taken out of my grandfather's thigh after being wounded in the battle of the Somme in the First World War. As a tiny child, one of my most vivid memories is sitting on his lap and being shown this precious box. I did not understand much then, and it is a great sadness that by the time I did my grandfather had died, but I learned about the horses in the mud and the bully beef and above all I understood the wonder of the wound which had got him off the Somme and back to the safety of Blighty! It is a daily miracle that we and this fragile planet are here at all and if that shrapnel had found its target differently, killing my grandfather, then my dad and I would never have lived; the unique person that I am would never have been.

So each person is special beyond special and encounter with them wakes us up. Deep encounters always transform us; they extend our world. If we engage deeply with another person we are taken into their experience of life. We begin to see things as they see them: their assumptions, their dreams, their pain, their longing, and as we do this we are forced to question our own way of seeing. We are woken up to new possibilities. This is beautifully expressed in Thomas Ogletree's book *Hospitality to the Stranger*:

> Strangers have stories to tell which we have never heard before, stories which can redirect our seeing ... Their stories invite us to see the world from a novel perspective ... The stranger does not simply challenge or subvert our assumed world of meaning: she may enrich, even transform, that world.[9]

So each person has a world of wonder to share with us and we can be awoken by them.

Once at church in Oxford, I was deeply aware of the line of people going up for communion. Suddenly each person seemed to me imbued with a deep specialness and I was moved to tears as I watched. People rushed to care for me and I found myself unable to explain that I was not weeping for pain but with joy and thankfulness. Years later there was a moment of recognition when reading Thomas Merton's *Confessions of a Guilty Bystander* in which he wrote: 'There is no way of telling people that they are all walking around shining like the sun.'[10]

If this can be so for us, how much more for Jesus, the Son of God. Kierkegaard describes Jesus as 'having eternity in him'. Indeed it is in Christ that we catch a glimpse of what eternity is about and this was no more so than in the extraordinary event which we call the Transfiguration,[11] an event which filled the disciples to the full with wonder and awe. To understand the Transfiguration it helps to put this extraordinary event in context. It follows hard on the heels of the great recognition scene where Peter confesses that Jesus is the Christ,[12] but also of two predictions of how Jesus must suffer and die. The Christ whom Peter has recognised will not go up to glory before he has suffered and died. Of course the disciples are not stupid and by now would have gathered that it is risky to follow Jesus; just look what had happened to John the Baptist. But this was different. What Jesus seemed to be saying was that it was not just that dangers were around but that Jesus would and must walk straight into them. This is no risky gamble which might come off; it *is* going to lead to suffering and to death for certain. Jesus has to walk this way and they need to begin to understand.

I was reminded of this when I was recently taken to my first football match by my son-in-law, Anton. It was freezing cold and I think I was the only one of the 88,000 crowd wrapped in a blanket, but I enjoyed it. It occurred to me that what we have just been describing would have been a bit like a pre-match announcement to the assembled fans, all buoyed up for victory, that their team was going to let in the first five attempts at goal, come what may. You bet all hell would break loose!

The idea that Jesus must walk acceptingly to his death, this kind of defeat was just not in the disciples' plans. As the cartoon character Charlie Brown once said: 'Winning ain't everything but losing ain't anything!' Well ... quite!

No wonder this calls forth a strong negative reaction

from Peter who grabs Jesus in protest. Messiahs don't just give up and get killed by the authorities; indeed that would simply prove that Jesus was not the Messiah. This to Peter was all confusing and deeply upsetting. However, suffering and death are this Messiah's way; it is Jesus' vocation and destiny and no one must block them. Even the rebuke of Peter, Jesus' right-hand man, cannot be tolerated. Peter must stop thinking like a mere mortal, stop seeing the world's take on reality and start to wake up to God's reality. In this, Peter, James and John are about to have a crash course. They are given a glimpse of Jesus' identification with God. Philippians 2 talks of Jesus giving up all privilege to become human but in this encounter on the mountain it seems as though the glory which he has given up comes streaming through. It can no longer be hidden for it is Jesus' reality, and the three chosen disciples are filled with wonder and awe as they witness this. This extreme dose of God's reality jolts them awake from the world's reality, the one which so recently Peter was defending. They see the kingdom of God in all its power and glory, and Jesus, for a moment, as he truly is in his full majesty. They don't know what to do, so they wonder about building tabernacles![13]

Soon, it has passed and all is back to normal, but the disciples never will be. They will never be able to forget or want to forget this extraordinary experience. They have been filled with wonder, seeing Jesus transfigured, transformed and this glimpse into God's reality as it really is will transform them too. Before long, they come down the mountain and straight back into a storm. A huge crowd was standing around the rest of the disciples and the religious scholars were cross-examining them about a demon-possessed boy whom the disciples had failed to help. Normal life beckoned and from now on they were to be tested to their limit and beyond.

I am writing this on a January day with a blizzard outside my window and recollecting a retreat when we were reflecting on the Transfiguration. On the Saturday morning we awoke at Shepherds Dene, a beautiful retreat house amongst the wonderful landscape of Northumberland, to find it covered in snow, glinting in the bright sunshine and set against a deep blue sky. This landscape was transformed, transfigured. We were almost speechless with wonder. At the final Eucharist the next day people were invited to bring something as their reflection on the retreat. One man brought a Tupperware container filled with snow. I shall always remember what he said: 'The snow has beautifully transformed the landscape but it will melt. The snow in my box will melt, but the melting will produce water which will sustain our ordinary lives. So moments of transfiguration can change us but they do not last forever, we cannot prolong the experience as Peter wanted to by building his shelters. What we can do is take the essence of them into our ordinary lives, the water from the snow so to speak and let it sustain us.'[14] The disciples had been amazed by wonder and they would never be the same again.

J. V. Taylor calls the moments of transcendence which this reflection has been exploring 'annunciations', which seems an excellent word as they are about the act or process of announcing. They speak of things beyond themselves and awaken us to the reality which is always there but constantly evades our gaze. They announce to us that there is something beyond the everyday sights and sounds of our lives, something altogether bigger and other than our daily experience. A reality to which we are awoken by wonder and which helps us to keep our eyes open and our minds awake. This is well put in Veronica Zundel's poem:

I scan you on the figured page
In tales of every distant age
And chant you in a holy song
But yet I hear, I see you wrong

I am so small
You are so all …

For narrow is my inward sight
I do not spell your meanings right
And guttering my outward gaze
I do not steady trace your ways

My steps are small
To map your all

Then break me wide your raging word
In flintstruck light from darkness stirred
And break me wide your dancing love
That soars the hawk, that swoops the dove

I am so small
You are so all in all.[15]

FOR DISCUSSION

1. The 3-year-old Ben was filled with wonder at the sight of terraced houses going down to the river (p.45)! What fills you with wonder?

2. Have you ever had an experience like the ones described by the author and J.V. Taylor (p.44)? What happened?

3. What feelings were associated with it?

4. Why do we often find it difficult to really be present in response to the wonder of the world? What distracts us?

5. In the light of what the author shares about clouds and rivers how do you respond to what Graham Swift wrote: 'Why should there be certain things in this random universe which cry out to us with their loveliness?' (p.47).

6. The author argues that poetry, art, drama and music can lead us to wonder and to wake up to a deeper reality. What experiences if any do you have of this?

7. Do you agree with the author that there are certain times in our lives when we are more open to wonder? When has this been so for you?

8. How do you react to Dennis Potter's idea of 'nowness'?

9. Using the experience of her grandfather in the First World War the author says that 'the probability of our particular existence is billions to one.' How do you feel about that?

10. Each person has a world of wonder to share with us and we can be awoken by them. How do you respond to the following quotation from Thomas Ogletree: 'Strangers have stories to tell which we have never heard before, stories which redirect our seeing ... Their stories invite us to see the world from a novel perspective ... The stranger does not simply challenge or subvert our assumed world of meaning: she may enrich, even transform, that world.'

BIBLE PASSAGE FOR REFLECTION: MATTHEW 17:1-9

1. Do you share the disciples' confusion that Jesus must walk the way of suffering and of death?

2. What do you make of the crash course in reality which Peter, James and John received on the mountain top?

3. Does Kierkegaard's description of Jesus as 'having eternity in him' help us understand what is going on?

4. Have you ever had a particularly powerful experience of God's presence? How did this change you?

5. How do you respond to the story about the snow at Shepherd's Dene (p.55)? Does the idea that mountain-top experiences always fade but can feed us in our everyday life make sense to you? Can you give any examples in your own life?

CLOSING PRAYER

Lord of life,
your life embraces me on
every side;
I open my arms to greet you.
God, grant me a clearer vision
of the many-splendoured thing,
your presence in and through all things,
that I may be one with your mind of love.

Richard Harries, *Praying Round the Clock*
(Mowbray, 1983)

4

WAKING UP TO DEATH

There was never much of a time when I did not have to deal in some way with death. My mother had been orphaned at the age of seven and I always knew this was an awful thing to bear. As a result of this she was brought up by her grandparents and when I was growing up my great grandfather, Poppy as I called him, had always lived with us. When I was also seven, Poppy died. To a child's mind this was very difficult to grasp; that this lovely, kind man who had dried my hair in front of the fire, let me play and climb trees while he did his allotment and had comforted and reassured me when my mother was late home from shopping ... that he was gone and would never come back ... how could this be? That I would never see him again and that no one really knew where he was ... how could this be? Of course there was talk of heaven but why was everyone so upset if that was true? I had gone to school as usual and death had just come and taken Poppy and there was, it seemed, nothing to be done. He had not even said 'Goodbye' to me! The completeness of the vanishing was difficult to get my head around, as was the fact of it. That people knew this could happen, indeed would happen, and yet they could get on with life seemed remarkable. I kept on the lookout for Poppy for a long time. It deeply affected me this dying, leaving me terrified for years that if I was at school away from home someone would die and they would not have said 'Goodbye'.

So I was woken up to death early. My stark experience of death at a young age is in marked contrast to the world portrayed in television commercials: a world of eternal youth and no sign of death. All that matters, it seems, is that we stay alive and that we don't grow *old*! As long as we stay alert, avoid second-hand cigarette smoke, take the right pills, have cosmetic surgery when required, eat a healthy diet and drive carefully ... all will be well. Certainly we desperately want to believe so! However, the truth is that none of this really gets us very far. Real life is not about pretending to be immortal, that is complete nonsense. Real life is always lived in the face of death and by failing to attend to this reality we pay a very high price both individually and as a society. We pay particularly with our inability to plumb the depths of life, floating rather aimlessly over the surface, failing to explore life's real meaning.

Death is not an accidental occurrence at the end of an otherwise fine life. Death defines life! Many years ago whilst reading for an essay about death and dying I found this very helpful quotation which I have never forgotten: 'Here in an evolutionary universe death is a necessity. Birth and death give boundaries to our living, defining our experiences.'[1] Death, to put it another way, is like a question mark at the end of a sentence which actually determines the character of the whole sentence. Death is a dimension of everything which precedes it.'[2]

We can of course simply try to ignore death. We sleepwalk along and put off thinking about it for a rainy day! As the hero of Mark Haddon's novel says: 'The secret of contentment and happiness is to ignore many things completely,'[3] and this we do as we fill our heads with all manner of distractions. It is as if what we take for happiness is simply deferred despair and this when we all really know that death is skulking about. This is well evoked in the opening sentences of James Runcie's novel *Canvey Island*, which is based around the 1953 flood that devastated the east coast of Britain, leaving 307 people dead and 40,000 homeless:

I know the fear of death is always with us but sometimes it can disappear for days. You don't think about it when your child gives you a smile that you know is meant only for you or when the sea is dead calm and you're out fishing with no one to trouble you. You don't think about death, of course you don't, it never crosses your mind, but then back it comes, far too soon, telling you not to be so cocky, don't think this is going to last, mate, this is all the happiness you're going to get and you should be grateful I didn't come before.[4]

We all know, as this character knows, that death is there, lurking about and this knowledge can fill us with a sense of futility and despair. No wonder we try to block it out, but if our being fully alive is to be more than a

blissful illusion it must entail a capacity to face death.
If we can face death I believe that we will also face life
with less fear and more reality. Good Friday on first
appearance brings us to this same place of despair and
futility. This charismatic young man, so full of life and
love for God, so deeply loved himself, is hanging on a
cross being barbarically and painfully put to a lingering
death; this wholly innocent man betrayed, humiliated
and abandoned. What on earth is the point?

As Christians we believe there is a point to life;
that things are more than they seem. Bonhoeffer, the
German theologian, after being summoned to the
gallows by the Nazis, turned to his comrades and said:
'This is the end ... for us, the beginning of life.'[5]For
Bonhoeffer, the dying and rising of Christ meant that
we have to reinterpret death not as an enemy but as
a friend and not as the end but the beginning. If we
can begin to see death as the appropriate end to the
journey, as that which defines and makes sense of life,
then we can echo these words spoken by Cardinal Joseph
Bernardin: 'As a person of faith, I see death as a friend,
as a transition from earthly life to life eternal.'[6]

One of the lessons of life is to begin to see with the
eye of faith that in all situations there can be a path
which leads to a new and greater life. As we experience
this in our daily lives, 'it becomes less of a leap to trust
that even in the face of physical death God has provided
such a path'.[7] So life is about living life to the full. Not
seeking death, but seeking to live in such a way that death
is the logical next step. As Dag Hammarskjöld said in
his journal: 'Do not seek death. Death will find you.

But seek the road which makes death a fulfilment.'[8]

One monk headmaster is reputed to have disconcerted a group of the great and the good by telling them that he was not preparing his pupils for Oxbridge, the City or the Guards but for death. You can well imagine their response! It certainly seems bizarre on first hearing but the Christian view is that only those who begin to face the reality of death are able to start to live the fullness of life.[9]

Another image that I have found helpful (perhaps because I am a geographer!) is that of a stream starting out high up in the hills and making its way down to the sea. Its whole task is to cut down so that when it gets to the sea it will be at sea level not 100m above or below. Its task is to be ready to enter the sea when it reaches the appropriate place. Our task is similar, to live our lives in such a way that when we arrive at death we are ready to meet it. Christ lived his life in such a way. 'It is done!' A cry of triumph and I am sure a cry of relief. 'It is completed!' Literally it means 'It is perfected'. The journey is done!

For my beloved friend Sue, her journey was done last year. She had always experienced poor health and had suffered hugely in her life, not least from crippling bouts of depression, and yet, and maybe because of this, she was the most alive person I have ever met: full of laughter and joy. She had plumbed the depth of suffering and through this had developed the most profound compassion for people. She had walked with death and the possibility of death for years and finally after a very long illness took her own decision to refuse any further treatment. This meant that she knew she would die soon and she called her family and close friends to her bedside. I had visited the week before and we had discussed many things, including the sermon she wanted me to preach at her funeral. She helped me so much by looking death in the face and enabling me to talk about it and not be afraid. A very real gift! Then the final 'Good bye' arrived. What do you say? What do you do? How do you sum up the many years of deep love and friendship? How do you face the parting? Finally after we had talked and held each other it was time to leave. I stood at the door and looked at her and she looked back at me. I shrugged and said, 'There is no way to do this. How can I just walk out and leave you forever? There is no easy way to do this ... I just have to go.' So clumsy. So final. I opened the door and left and then in the ward I wept and wept and wept, knowing she was still there, but that I would never see her again in this life. In a very harsh way death is the end of a person and of their particular and unique life, but I fully believe that eternal life must mean that neither Sue nor her world is lost; that there is continuity beyond death of her individual life, but she is lost to me and so we encounter grief, one of the other great awakeners of life.

Our lives are shaped by grief, human mortality is absolutely reliable so grief is unavoidable and the more you love the more grief will come your way. How are our lives shaped by grief? What does the world look like when we are jolted awake from sleepwalking into this terrible reality? The deep agony of grief changes everything. It changes how we look at the past; joyful experiences become a sharp source of pain. It changes how we look at the present as our energy and joy in living evaporates and it changes the future which now seems empty, lonely and futile; damaged forever in a way which it seems can never be fixed. Wolterstorff writes in his powerful book about his son's untimely death:

> It is the *neverness* that is so *painful*. Never again to be here with us — never to sit with us at table, never to travel with us, never to laugh with us, never to embrace us as he leaves for school, never to see his brothers and sisters marry. All the rest of our lives we must live without him. Only our death can stop the pain of his death.[10]

Everything changes in an instant. Yet people mostly and miraculously come through it.

A number of our dear friends have had to face what I imagine most of us would agree is the worst kind of grief: the death of a child. Without exception, they have faced this with great courage and a trust and openness which have helped us all. We can see in them, a gift to us of their grief, a profound understanding of life and a degree of compassion which is a great blessing. Their grief, being jolted awake daily to the loss of their child, not being able to escape into sleepwalking, bears fruit for them and for their friends but no one would ever, ever ask it of them. It will be hard for them to sleepwalk again.

What do you most fear? I ask people this question in the Quiet Days I lead. Their replies are very honest and very varied: loneliness, a painful lingering death, shame or public humiliation, the early death of someone you love, the loss of a child, poverty, loss of mental faculties, to name but a few. Of course, we do everything to avoid these disasters: buy insurance policies, save for a rainy day, never catch a plane, go to the gym, give up smoking, eat a balanced diet, never let our child out of our sight; but, and this is the really frightening thing, despite all our best efforts, what we most fear can still happen. When we understand this we begin to grow up.

Our society is in many ways a hard place in which to grow up. We often behave as if the highest purpose in life is simply to stay alive as long as possible. We have seen the sad consequences of this in many a nursing home. It is also the case that simply extending physical life can lead to living life in a defensive and not a generous way: small, selfish, risk-averse, self-absorbed and asleep lives can be the result. We need to learn that the real purpose of our lives is to *live*. Martin Luther King lived in this way. He lived a wide-awake life, living with the threat of death every day for many years until the day when he was assassinated. He came to see that he could not be himself if he allowed the threat of death to control him. He said this: 'The main thing is not how long I live but how well I have acquitted myself in the discharge of those truths which are high, noble and good.'[11]

Fully vibrant living it seems is only possible when

we are awake to the reality of death. There is, however, a balance required which it is hard to attain: enough awareness of death so that we live our lives awake to this possibility but not so much awareness that we are overwhelmed and unable to live the life which we have been given.

In his Letter to the Philippians the apostle Paul gives us what seems like a masterclass in coming to terms with death. It certainly leaves me standing. In prison in Rome, awaiting his trial and facing the very real possibility of execution, he has plenty of time to think and pray. Most of us would have been praying for rescue and release, and Paul had experienced God's rescue before, but this is not how he feels. He would rather the situation ended with his death for then he would be where he most longed to be, with his beloved Christ:

> For to me, to live is Christ and to die is gain. If I am to go on living in this body, this will mean fruitful labour for me. Yet what shall I choose? I do not know! I am torn between the two: I desire to depart and to be with Christ, which is better by far; but it is more necessary for you that I remain in the body.[12]

For most of us Christ is a compelling possibility but not such a reality that we would easily give up this life on earth. For Paul, Christ was a shining reality which put all other things in the dark; Christ was Paul's whole life. He fully believed that the full enjoyment of Christ lay beyond death and this he was eager to gain.

As I write this I admit to feeling bewildered. I read Paul's words and know that in some deep sense he must be right. If not, what do we have to live for and proclaim now? But I find myself far from being able to utter Paul's words. I confess to often feeling more at home with our society's view that death is the ultimate disaster to be evaded at all costs rather than to be willingly embraced. Why are we so afraid to die? For me, as I think about it, it is a lot about loss: loss of all that is known and secure, loss of love, loss of family and friends, loss of the earth's stunning beauty. I suppose I am also really afraid of making the journey on my own. What I think we are asked to grasp is that all that we fear losing is really only a faint foretaste of heaven itself, a foretaste of a coming home where there will be no more loss.

> 'Never again will they hunger;
> never again will they thirst.
> The sun will not beat upon them,
> Nor any scorching heat.
> For the Lamb at the centre of the throne will be their shepherd;
> He will lead them to springs of living water.
> And God will wipe away every tear from their eyes.'[13]

No wonder Paul was impatient to die, impatient to wake up in God's reality beyond this heartbreakingly beautiful but tragically incomplete world.

Loss awakens us to these realities and life trains us in loss whether we want it to or not. Gradually we need to come closer to God's reality, closer to Christ, to get to the place where we can begin to embrace dying as gain. This task of letting go is very hard, we struggle to do it. It is a lifelong process and one that we are learning until the end. Love is tried and tested and proved in the letting go and life brings us there time and time again: letting go of parents, letting go of ambitions, letting go of children, letting go of securities, letting go of the past, letting go of our countless possessions, letting go of loved ones, letting go of resentment and letting go of status and power, letting go of being physically strong and fit. The following two poems help us to reflect upon this:

> You must be able
> to do three things:
> to love what is mortal,
> to hold it
> against your bones,
> knowing your own life
> depends on it;
> and when the time comes
> to let it go,
> to let it go.[14]

Another poem, by Norman MacCaig, called 'Small Boy', takes us to the same place:

> He picked up a pebble
> And threw it in the sea.
> And another, and another.

He couldn't stop.
He wasn't trying to fill the sea.
He wasn't trying to empty the beach.
He was just throwing away,
Nothing else but.
Like a kitten playing
He was practising for the future
When there'll be so many things
He'll want to throw away
If only his fingers will unclench
And let them go.[15]

Trusting God and letting go is a lifelong learning which will continue to death; the big letting go of ourselves or of those whom we love. The final words of Jesus challenge us here. They are the psalmist's words set in the Jewish prayer book to be said before falling asleep:

Father, into your hands I commend my spirit.
Father, I place my life into your hands.

It is the simplest, most childlike form of faith. Jesus often spoke of such trust in God's overarching power and goodness as the only true way to live and, of course, to die.

Henri Nouwen, to whose writing I owe a great debt, had a fascination for circuses and particularly for trapeze acts. He describes how trapeze acts are made up of two roles: the flyers and the catchers. Of course the flyers look like the stars as they risk life and limb careering through the air, but one of the flyers said to Henri Nouwen that the flyer does nothing and the catcher does everything. (I confess that this 'nothing' is not something for which I am going to volunteer!) The flyer explained: 'When I fly to the catcher I have simply to stretch out my arms and hands and wait for him to catch me and pull me to safety over the catch bar ... A flyer must fly and a catcher must catch, and the flyer must trust with outstretched arms that his catcher will be there for him.'

So often we measure our identity and success by how well we remain in control but in the end the final meaning of our lives will be determined more by our capacity to trust and our capacity to let go and to place ourselves into the hands of God. Dying and living it seems are both essentially about trusting in the catcher.[16]

Nothing I have written in this chapter is intended to negate the fact that death is an abomination against which we fight and, as the poet Dylan Thomas so aptly wrote, rage. Death is a great affront to love and grief is the price we pay for love. Is love then the answer to this affront? I trust so.

I have come into the hour of a white healing
Grief's surgery is over and I wear
The scar of my remorse and of my feeling ...

... I have come
Into the time when grief begins to flower
Into a new love ...
Now I have lost my loss ...

73

In some way I may later understand ...
And love I find has no considered end,

Nor is it subject to the wilderness
Which follows death. I am not traitor to
A person or a memory. I trace

Behind that love another which is running
Around, ahead. I need not ask its meaning.[17]

FOR DISCUSSION

1. The author shares her early experience of death at the beginning of this chapter. What is your earliest memory of death and can you identify with anything which is shared?

2. 'Here in an evolutionary universe death is a necessity. Birth and death give boundaries to our living, defining our experiences.' What do you make of this quotation from Lepp, especially in the light of some people's desire to live for ever, for example by deep-freezing their bodies?

3. How do you respond to this quotation from James Runcie's excellent novel *Canvey Island*: 'You don't think about death, of course you don't, it never crosses your mind but then back it comes, far too soon, telling you not to be so cocky, don't think this is going to last, mate, this is all the happiness you're going to get and you should be grateful I didn't come before?'

4. How do you respond to the monk headmaster who said he was not preparing pupils for Oxbridge, the City or the Guards but for death (p. 65)?

5. The author shares her experience of taking her

leave of her much-loved friend as she was dying. Have you had any similar experiences of taking your leave of the dying? How would you reflect on these experiences?

6. Wolterstorff writes in his very powerful book about the untimely death of his son in a climbing accident: 'It is the *neverness* that is so painful. *Never again* to be here with us, never to sit at table, never to laugh with us, never to embrace us ... All the rest of our lives we must live without him.' Does this chime in with your own experiences of grief?

7. Our society seems obsessed with not growing old and living for as long as possible. How does this compare with the following comment from Martin Luther King just before he was assassinated: 'The main thing is not how long I live but how well I have acquitted myself in the discharge of those truths which are high, noble and good'?

8. How do you respond to the poems about letting go (p. 71)? What experiences of letting go have you had to deal with and how did you cope?

9. An underlying theme to this whole chapter is grief. How if at all do you think the concept of 'letting go' informs our grief?

10. Do you find Henri Nouwen's illustration of the trapeze artists – the catcher and the flyer (p.72) – interesting or helpful?

BIBLE PASSAGE
FOR REFLECTION:
PHILIPPIANS 1:20-24

1. How do you respond to this passage from Philippians?
2. Why is it often difficult for us to react in this way to death?

CLOSING PRAYER

Gentle and mysterious God,
You gave me the gift of life.
And will be with me at my death;
I am afraid of dying suddenly, violently or painfully,
And I dread leaving behind those I love.
I give you my fears, as a gift of trust in you.
Help me to face the truth that we are all dying,
And let me remember
That if I can face up to my mortality with honesty,
I can live more fully now.

Angela Ashwin in *A Book of a Thousand Prayers*, p.217

5

WAKING UP TO LOVE

Sue, one of my closest friends, died last year, as I mentioned in the previous chapter.

She had asked me — perhaps it would be more accurate to say that she had required me — to speak at her funeral. As she was dying I was talking to her about the funeral. I asked her what she would want said of herself. She was very ill and weak and it was a great effort to answer. She said very quietly, 'She loved', then after much effort she repeated again, 'She loved.' It seems to me that love is what we are born for: to learn to love and to be loved by God and by other people. Our life's task is to become capable of loving and receiving love as St John of the Cross said, 'We shall be judged on love.'

Of all the many things we chase after and crave during our lifetime, love is really what matters. As we find ourselves beloved we find ourselves able to love in return and this is, of course, even more true of God's love for us. We have a lifetime to arrive at our own understanding that we are beloved of God and we need to be awoken to this reality. WilliamBlake claims that we are put on earth 'to learn to bear the beams of love'.[1] This is our life's work, but we struggle to love, sometimes corrupting love and often making a complete mess of things. If this is our natural environment we do not seem very competent or confident in it. Perhaps of all life's experiences love wakes us up the most. All deep encounters of love leave their mark, sometimes sadly wounds, but never nothing. That would indeed be an insult to the power and nature of love!

Our society idolises 'in-loveness'. Falling in love, romantic love certainly occupies our imaginations and the imagination of our culture and whole industries are built on it. There is barely a pop song which does not have love as its context. At the hairdressers I am always given copies of *Hello!* magazine to read. I joke with the hairdresser that I need to catch up with the wonderful stories of passionate falling in love this month before I come the next month and have to read about the divorces of the same couples and their new love attachments. All very exhausting! In-loveness is the diamond we seek. Falling in love is an ecstasy, a state of self-transcendence breaking into our lives and making us feel so alive. No one has ever loved like this before! Waking up from the sleepwalking of normal life is abrupt and absolute; suddenly everything is changed and transformed. You can always tell when someone is smitten because the name of the beloved is rarely off their lips or out of their thoughts; they cannot sleep for love or eat for love or think for love. Lovers are like a magnet to each other, always having to part too soon and always being too long apart. Love comes upon us and seems beyond our control; it happens to us in a seemingly

inevitable way, captured well by this Wendy Cope
poem:

My heart has made its mind up
And I'm afraid it's you.
Whatever you've got lined up,
My heart has made its mind up
And if you can't be signed up
This year, next year will do.
My heart has made its mind up
And I'm afraid it's you.[2]

In addition to the inevitability, being in love gives us a
feeling of rightness not just with the beloved but with
the whole world. We are wide awake; we see everything
differently: how have we missed the smell of newly cut
grass and the shouts of children playing, the birdsong
and the falling rain. Nothing can limit us; we feel that
we can be the very best person we hold the potential to
be. We can be deeply and profoundly connected with
another, we can seem as one and for a time we think we
are! In-loveness comes unbidden, shaking us awake. As
David Ford describes it in his inspiring book *The Shape
of Living*, a new person 'crosses the threshold of our lives
and overwhelms us'.[3]

We will never be the same again! We are bursting
with life. Such is love's impact that, as the poet Micheal
O'Siadhail writes, it 'shifts the boundaries of our
being'.[4] Life in a blink of an eye is simplified down to
one pursuit, one purpose: the beloved. It has its own
imperative and authority and demands to be put first

with sometimes disastrous effects. We are not easily in control of love. It can happen anytime and anywhere. No person is entirely love proof; however hard we try to protect ourselves a spark can land and begin to set a fire raging. The strange thing is that it is all too possible for the imperative of in-loveness to make us act against love. A married minister realised he had fallen in love with a woman in his congregation. He needed help and went to some, as he thought, wise friends. They were kind, but shocked. The conversation went roughly like this:

'You know that this is wrong.'

'Yes.'

'You know you should love your wife.'

'Yes.'

'You know this is not what God wants for you?'

'Yes.'

'So you must stop loving this woman.'

'Yes.'

This was followed by a prayer which was offered on his behalf to give up his feelings for her. He returned back to his church, now also burdened by having prayed to God that he would give up this love; a prayer he had not yet felt able to make. He could not do it just like that. This love was a powerful thing, a delightful thing, and his marriage was far from happy. He felt such guilt at breaking his promise to God that he sought no more help and had a full-blown affair, which ended in disaster. That was when he became my client.

I tell this story, with the man's permission of course, because it shows how complicated awakening in love can be. How do we deal with such an overwhelming emotion and work out our existing obligations? The advice he was given treated this too lightly. He needed continual help and freedom to find his way. So in-loveness can hijack us with disastrous effect.

Problematically, of course, people can fall in love a number of times in their lives. Each time in-loveness speaks with its own imperative and authority but sadly in-loveness is fickle. It cannot deliver the grandiose claims it makes for itself because it is so fragile. We find that we cannot sustain this level of emotional intensity. We fall out of love too, which is another major awakening from a different kind of sleepwalking, and when we do, we can be appalled at what we have done in love's name. I remember the married minister saying, 'But that's not like me, I'm not like that', as he had to face up to the devastation he had wreaked in his marriage, his family and his congregation. Human in-loveness tries to give us what only God can give; to bear what only God can bear.

As a priest, I am given the immense privilege of marrying people. At weddings I sometimes say something like: 'Today I can see you are in love which is as it should be. Today you are going to make some promises which will not be tested now or probably for a while. They will begin to be tested when one day you wake up and you are not quite so fully in love! Obviously today you are not promising to stay in love; you cannot after all promise a feeling. You are promising to act in love come what may, even and maybe especially when you don't feel it.' This often provokes a lot of conversation afterwards, not from the newlyweds but from older others who know the truth of this. I love these words of Pelagia's father in Louis de Bernières' novel *Captain Corelli's Mandolin*. He says:

> Love is a temporary madness, it erupts like volcanoes and then it subsides. And when it subsides you have to make a decision. You have to work out whether your roots have become so entwined together that it is inconceivable that you should ever part. Because that is what love is. Love is not breathlessness, it is not excitement ... No ... that is just being in love, which any fool can do. Love itself is what is left over when being in love has burned away. It doesn't sound very exciting but it is.[5]

We do not learn to love by day dreaming, being swept along by in-loveness. Love is learned through acts of love, the capacity for love is built through acts of love, repeated daily and which help to establish the habit of loving. Love is learned in a thousand upon thousand small moments when we decide to act in love or not. We are found wanting by I Corinthians 13: 'Love is patient, love is kind. It does not envy. It does not boast, it is not proud. It is not rude, it is not self-seeking, it is not easily angered, it keeps no record of wrongs. Love does not delight in evil but rejoices with the truth. It always protects, always trusts, always hopes, always perseveres.'[6] To attain this will give most of us more than a lifetime's work! Having written *Struggling to be Holy* I find myself often being asked to go and speak about holiness. I always point out that the book is about struggling to be holy and that I know much more about struggling than about being holy!

Being holy has sometimes seemed much too big an ask for me and so I decided a couple of years ago to try to be kind. It seemed more manageable. I have to confess to never having lived a completely kind day yet. I am challenged by the struggle I find in myself to simply be kind: to choose not to say that seemingly innocuous thing which I know will hurt, to not put someone down to put myself up, to give the help which is needed without being grumpy and put upon. So one of the building blocks of I Corinthians 13 is proving more than enough to keep me going. Learning to love is a practical bit-by-bit activity full of choices to make. I think Jesus was thinking of this in Matthew 25, 'For I was hungry and you gave me something to eat, I was thirsty and you gave me something to drink, I was a stranger and you invited me in, I needed clothes and you clothed me, I was sick and you looked after me, I was in prison and you came to visit me.'[7] So love is not just a feeling, it reveals itself in action. Some of the people whom I most respect are those who day by day and week by week act out this love in action: being Samaritans, visiting people in prison, caring for the elderly, running food banks, or coming alongside troubled families. This love is not trumpeted and celebrated like in-loveness or family love but is profoundly of God. It is a love which keeps faith even when no love is being offered back.

The Hasidic masters tell the story of the rabbi who disappeared every Shabat Eve, 'to commune with God in the forest' as his congregation thought. So one Sabbath night they deputed one of their cantors to follow the rabbi and observe the holy encounter. Deeper and deeper into the woods the rabbi went until he came to the small cottage of an old Gentile woman, sick to death and crippled into a painful posture. Once there, the rabbi cooked for her and carried her firewood and swept her floor. Then when the chores were finished, he returned immediately to his little house next to the synagogue. Back in the village the people demanded of the one they'd sent to follow him, 'Did the rabbi go up to heaven as we thought?' 'Oh no,' the cantor answered after a thoughtful pause, 'our rabbi went much higher than that.'[8]

It is always a huge risk to love; to entrust our vulnerability and frailty to the precarious depths of another's vulnerability and frailty. When someone entrusts their vulnerability and frailty to us are we up to it? Will we let them down? Will they let us down? When someone we love deeply hurts us, it is one of the worst and most painful things that can happen. The extent of the hurt is a measure of how vital that person is to us. If we have let them become deeply part of us and then the relationship goes wrong our whole being is threatened; we will find we are fighting for our lives. We can only be most cruelly hurt when we have most freely given. It can be tempting to sleepwalk so that we protect ourselves against such hurt but it is essential that we be woken up from living life in avoidance of love.

The vulnerability of being in love is as nothing in my view to the vulnerability of being a parent. I remember recently a very new dad saying to me in hospital that it was all going great, but that he could not wait to get home to get back to normal. I smiled back and nodded and thought to myself that things will never get back to normal! Having a baby changes us forever as I have no doubt he will very soon discover. It is a most effective way of being woken up from the sleepwalking of our everyday life. We find ourselves overwhelmed: the intense emotions of wonder as we look at the tiny, beautifully formed body, the feelings of love and anxiety as we realise the immensity of the gift of this new person into our lives and of course the huge upheaval in our lifestyles. Truly things will never be the same again.

To be a parent is to accept, in a most profound way, a stranger into the very heart of our lives to share our life forever. Whatever that child does, wherever they go, whatever they become they will always be there in our hearts for good or bad. Being a parent requires nothing less from us than everything. It is a huge commitment as we care for a child, guide a child, protect and challenge a child and for certain we will find ourselves deeply wanting. Being a truly loving parent is a work that guarantees our own transformation. It will bring us time and time again to the limits of our selfishness; our own smallness is continually made apparent. To give a trivial example: I have always had a rather quick and sharp temper when provoked or tired. I have always hated this and during my twenties I felt, somewhat smugly, that I had got it sorted and that my sunny nature would prevail. On becoming a parent however I discovered that my capacity to lose my temper was still hugely intact. What I had actually done was to conform my context to suit me so that there were not many situations which caused me to have a short fuse. My children's arrival and the total disruption of my life very soon taught me otherwise!

I personally found all the practical changes of parenthood totally disorientating. I don't think I was ever cut out for the care of babies, but for me the main change was being made vulnerable in a new and overwhelming way; a way I could never have imagined. We become unprotected as far as our children are concerned. We all try to be 'good' parents but because we are damaged ourselves we cannot be the perfect parents we long to be and, of course, we damage our own children in turn. Being a parent is a massive wake-up call. It re-orientates our lives. 'The world of your children takes up the horizon of your heart.'[9] We are made so vulnerable by this deep and overwhelming love. The work of parenthood is full of delight but full too of risk with no guarantees at all of the outcome or what will be asked of us on the way or how much we will be found wanting in the task. What is certain is that we will be as profoundly shaped by this encounter of love as our children will be – probably more.

This whole experience is, of course, a way of being woken up to the nature of God's love for us. I shall never forget while I was training for ordination reading Vanstone's wonderful book *Love's Endeavour, Love's Expense*. It woke me up to the precarious nature of God's love for his creation. God is always striving with all his effort to love us and longing to draw forth our free response of love to him. But as with parental love nothing is guaranteed. Love cannot be demanded, simply offered. Authentic love always gives the object of love a certain power over us. So, as the book says, God's endeavour of love towards his creation is a risk which can always be met with either 'triumph or tragedy'. God's activity of love must always be perilous; its security lying not in its certainty of outcome but in the unconditional, unsparing love of God who will not abandon a single scrap of his creation. God is love, the very nature of God is love and therefore he can do no other than love; an unsparing love which is shown above all in the authentic, generous love of Christ.[10]

Believing as I do in the vulnerability of God's love and our freedom of response, I have always been bemused by the commandment in Mark 12:31 to 'Love the Lord your God with all your heart and with all your soul and with all your mind and with all your strength. The second is this: love your neighbour as yourself. There is no commandment greater than these.'[11] Being commanded to love seems bonkers! You can command obedience but you can never command love; surely by its nature it has to be freely given. Command implies an element of fear in the one being commanded which would seem to have no place in a loving relationship. I have been helped to understand this commandment in a different way in a sermon by Martin Smith who sees the command not so much to rebellious humanity who withhold, but to reticent humanity who cannot bring themselves to believe that God loves them:

So what is the clue to the puzzle? If you read between the lines, God is saying something like this: 'Look, if you really knew who I am, the intensity of my beauty, the allure of my glory, the attraction of my love, you would be totally caught up in love. But the trouble is, you would hold back. You would disqualify yourself. You would ridicule yourself for presuming to think you could be my lover. So I have to tell you, I have to command you! Come to me! Don't hold back! Don't settle for obedience, for religious observance, for conformity! Let yourself go. Go the whole way! Love me! Nothing less will satisfy my love for you!'[12]

We struggle to understand the nature of the relationship which is offered. It is so unequal that we are astonished and scared and we want to hide, feeling utterly unworthy. Yet the only way we can love God is in relationship, so God works tirelessly to draw us in, always offering us a profound and intimate relationship. God's insistence and our reluctance is wonderfully expressed in George Herbert's much-loved poem:

Love bade me welcome; yet my soul drew back,
Guilty of dust and sin.
But quick-eyed Love, observing me grow slack
From my first entrance in,
Drew nearer to me, sweetly questioning,
If I lack'd any thing.

A guest, I answer'd, worthy to be here:

Love said, You shall be he.
I the unkind, ungrateful? Ah, my dear
I cannot look on thee.
Love took my hand, and smiling did reply,
Who made the eyes but I?

Truth, Lord, but I have marr'd them: let my shame
Go where it doth deserve.
And know you not, says Love, who bore the blame?
My dear, then I will serve.
You must sit down, says Love, and taste my meat:
So I did sit and eat.[13]

The other thing which has always worried me about this commandment is 'loving your neighbour as yourself'. It seems to me that most of us don't much love ourselves so it would be rather a raw deal for our neighbours. I remember a man who had come to me for counselling because he had been suffering from depression for much of his life. He was trying to convince me that he was rubbish, he loathed himself, felt that he was worth nothing. One day I was visiting a church with friends and in the church hall where we went to have coffee I was stunned by the beauty and artistry of a huge mural covering nearly all of one wall; it was wonderful and life-giving. I was further stunned to know it was the work of my client. In my next session with him I shared how moved I had been by his work. He simply said, 'Oh that's nothing; it doesn't count, it's just painting.'

When we don't love ourselves then no evidence will prove that we are lovable and have real gifts to share.

So there are problems because we do not love ourselves enough, but there are also problems because we are trapped in self-love; preoccupied with ourselves, me, me, me, with our prisons of comfort and security. Most of us extend the walls to include a chosen few family and friends but it is still self-love, simply an extended version! In his autobiography, Thomas Merton captures the superficial attraction of loving ourselves for ourselves. Four years after leaving school and having experienced many of the distractions of our contemporary world, he writes: 'I had become a true child of the modern world completely tangled up in petty and useless concerns with myself, and almost incapable of even considering or understanding anything that was really important to my own true interests ... In filling myself, I had emptied myself. In grasping things, I had lost everything. In devouring pleasures and joys, I had found distress and anguish and fear.'[14]

It is clear that self-preoccupation does not lead to happiness and a self-preoccupied person is someone most of us would avoid like the plague. It is all too easy to co-opt God into this arrangement to meet our overblown requirements and we can fall into treating God as if he is just there to meet our needs. Life offers us a gradual movement away from these distorted images of self, either of preoccupied self-love or self-loathing. We need to be repeatedly woken up from these distortions and this happens sometimes dramatically and sometimes gently, but always as we reach out to connect with others. As we encounter others it helps us to grow in self-awareness and to develop a more realistic love and acceptance of who we really are. There is much of self-illusion to be rid of and a false self to be taken off but as we begin to get glimpses of our true self there is a recognition that it has always been there. As we begin to see ourselves through God's eyes we can begin to drop the part of ourselves that we present to the world and start to love the real self. It is this self, our true self, created by God and what God longs for us to become, that is the self we are commanded to love.

I cannot write of finding our true selves through love without mentioning friendship. I wrote about friendship at length in my previous book but need to nod to its importance here. In our society it is certainly the poor relation among the other loves we have already mentioned, and wrongly so. Deep friendship requires the meeting of equals. I have several friends who have accompanied me throughout much of my life and they are as gold to me. They are like the glue which holds my life together: they look out for me; they will kick me into touch if necessary; they laugh with me and cry with me. I try to share my truth with my friends. They are diverse and meet different parts of me and I am confident that they love me as I love them. They underpin all the rest of my life; all the rest of my loving. I would be utterly lost without them and will go to much trouble to meet up with them.

St Augustine called life 'a road of the affections', a process of learning what is worthy of love and learning how to live appropriately. All our experiences of love are like wake-up calls. Like looking through a crack in a door into a room beyond, which we know holds something of God's wider love. All love in this life as lovers-in-the-making is a sample and foretaste of the 'real thing'; a sample and foretaste of the kingdom of God whose way of being is such as to challenge and defeat all our normal ways of understanding reality. This is beautifully portrayed in R. S. Thomas's poem entitled 'The Kingdom' where he describes how the consumptive is healed and the blind look at themselves in mirrors in which they can see again. He tells us that this kingdom is a long way off but:

> ... to get
> There takes no time and admission
> Is free, if you purge yourself with
> Your need only and the simple offering
> Of your faith, green as a leaf.[15]

Using different images and parables to challenge our preconceptions of reality, Jesus was determined to make us think about the nature of God's love. In Luke 15 we find probably the best-known parable (only the Good Samaritan is a serious rival), which at my Sunday school was always called 'The Prodigal Son'.[16] I had no idea whatsoever what the word 'prodigal' even meant! Maybe it would be more accurate to call it 'The Tale of Two Sons' as it is at least as much about the elder son, or even more aptly, 'The Tale of the Loving Father' as it is quintessentially about the proclamation of God's love and mercy.

We are challenged in this parable to choose between

the realities of our view of the world and the realities of the kingdom of God. In this parable the tensions are focused around our notion of 'just deserts' and the exercise of the love and generosity of God. We know the story well, too well perhaps: the conflict between the two brothers, one worthy, diligent and hardworking with expectations of what is the proper and earned reward for his work; the other one the waster, the hedonist who also has expectations but runs out of money and eventually has very little expectation at all. It is he, of course, who wakes up. There are two quite different perceptions at work through these characters; two different realities. There is one reality in which 'just deserts' is the king and the other in which 'generous love' is the king. The point for us, of course, is that if 'just deserts' were truly king we would all lose our heads, each and every one of us. So we are naturally drawn to the great tenderness of the father going out in love to meet his wayward child, but most of us are also, if we are honest, at least a bit irked by a sense of unfairness.

The problem with the older brother is, in a way, his lack of tenderness. He seems to have no joy at all in his brother's return. Does he love him? It certainly does not seem so. The generosity of the father serves in fact to expose the true nature of the elder brother's hard work. It exposes the evil in his heart, the envy, the greed, the jealousy, the anger. It lays bare the fact that he has not been working in grateful response to his father's tender love for him, but out of a self-interested duty. He is, after all, as his father gently reminds him, supervising his own patrimony.

('My son, everything I have is yours.') Somewhere deep down he does believe that he is worthy enough to merit his father's love. Jesus is trying to make it clear that any version of 'worthiness' is inappropriate because it is operating in the wrong dimension, the wrong understanding of reality. No one by human desert can enter the kingdom of heaven; it is God's love and grace which determine the rewards, and he seems to be particularly generous to those who do not see themselves as deserving. We only need to recall the Parable of the Workers in the Vineyard[17] in Matthew chapter 20 to get this in focus: the vineyard owner who pays all the workers the same amount regardless of how long or how hard they have worked. It really is a very trying parable indeed and it starts 'The kingdom of heaven is like ...'. Again we are to understand that we need to wake up to God's reality, to God's kingdom which is so very different from our own understanding of reality. Both these parables represent a systematic subversion of our world of conventional wisdom.

The father's love is the key for both his sons. His action in leaving the banquet and pleading with the elder son is paralleled in the story with the father running out to hug and kiss the younger son. Both sons through their different actions have excluded themselves but to both the father goes out in great tenderness. There is no rejection of the worth of either son, but only the one who has been woken up by his experiences of life, who has been stripped even of the basic essentials and has become an outcast is able to respond to the love which is offered. He has spent some time alone with himself and has begun to see things, especially himself, as they really are.

I was challenged recently by a retelling of this story by Trevor Dennis in a modern setting: younger son goes off on Suzuki, lives the high life in London and ends up as a porter at Clapham Junction. (Do they still have porters at Clapham Junction?) Anyway, the last straw is the cockroach in his tea, so back he comes. Yes ... yes, we know the story. I will let Trevor Dennis take it up in his own words:

Four days after leaving Clapham Junction he arrived on foot. You will remember he no longer had the motorbike, and the buses were on strike. His father saw him as he appeared slowly over the brow of the hill, and he ran, despite the stiffness of his legs – well, your legs would have been stiff if you had stood watching for as long as he had – he ran to meet him. As he approached him the father cried out, 'My son, my son! You're home!' and went to fling his arms around him. But the son walked up to him, dealt him a vicious blow to the jaw and kicked him into the ditch, and marched on to help himself to the rest of his father's estate.

He did not look back. Had he done so, he would have seen his father crawl out of the ditch, and he would have seen too the empty embrace and the lips moving in silent words of blessing.[18]

This ending threw me. I found it shocking as it shows that love can be rejected and that the one who loves can be deeply hurt. I don't know how you reacted. Would the father still love? I wasn't sure and felt pushed a bit too far. If the son was guilty and wanted to say sorry, all well and good; I could deal with that. But if the son had learned nothing, was unrepentant and was full of hatred could I accept that? I sadly recognise in myself a deep resistance to such free-flowing love and forgiveness. Can God really love him or me like that? It put me in mind of this observation from the mystic Julian of Norwich which I have always found very challenging:

Some of us believe that God is all powerful and is able to do everything and that he is all wise and knows how to do everything. But as for believing that he is all love and will do everything, there we hold back. And this lack of faith is what hinders God's lovers most, as I see it.[19]

FOR DISCUSSION

1. Do you think, as St John of the Cross states, that 'we shall be judged on love'? What do you think that means?

2. The book states that our society idolises 'in-loveness'. Do you agree? Can you give some examples?

3. How do you respond to the book's description of falling in love? Do you agree with the idea that 'in-loveness' comes unbidden and, as the poet Micheal O'Siadhail says, 'shifts the boundaries of our being'?

4. What would you want to say to a newly married couple about love? (p.84)

5. How do you respond to what the book says about parental love? Can you give examples of how the demands of parental life might be transformational? (p.87)

6. What do you make of Vanstone's idea that God's endeavour of love towards his creation is a risk which will either be met with triumph or tragedy? (p.89)

7. Do you think that we underestimate the importance

of love in friendship? Why do you think this might be? (p.93)

8. God's insistence to love and our reluctance to be loved by God is wonderfully expressed in George Herbert's poem 'Love bade me welcome'. Does this poem ring true in your experience? (p.90)

9. 'Love the Lord your God with all your heart and with all your soul and with all your mind and with all your strength' (Mark 12:31). What hinders us from doing this?

10. 'Love your neighbour as yourself.' Most of us struggle to love our neighbours and even more to love ourselves. What are the issues here? How do you respond to the story on p.92?

BIBLE PASSAGE FOR REFLECTION: LUKE 15:11-32

1. Do you agree that in this parable we are challenged to choose between our notion of 'just deserts' and the exercise of the love and generosity of God? Can you think of any other examples of this in the Gospels?
2. What are the the older son's problems?
3. What are the the younger son's problems?
4. Which of these two do you most identify with, and why?
5. The father's love is the key for both the sons. How did you respond to the passage from a modern-day retelling by Trevor Dennis (p.97)?

CLOSING PRAYER

God our lover,
in whose arms we are held,
and by whose passion we are known:
require of us also that love
which is filled with longing,
delights in the truth,
and costs not less than everything,
through Jesus Christ, Amen.

Janet Morley, *All Desires Known* (SPCK, 1992)

6

WAKING UP TO LIFE

I once heard an interesting interview on the radio with John Tavener, the composer. He had suffered a serious illness while in Switzerland which had landed him in intensive care and rendered him unconscious for a long time. They feared he was brain-dead, but one day, while his wife played him some Mozart, he lifted his hand to conduct. Gradually he recovered, although he was still in constant pain. This was clearly a major wake-up call. Tavener shared that, before this illness, he had lived only for music but afterwards, while music was still enormously important, he lived for his children in a way that he didn't before. He explained that the experience had changed him; making him more sensitive, more caring and more interested in others. This did not happen overnight; at first he felt wretched and could see no sense in anything, but gradually he began to see things differently. The illness and pain woke him up and helped him to open up his life in a way which did not seem possible before.

John Tavener's experience reminds me of a documentary on the effect that being held hostage had on people. We might reasonably expect people to come out of this experience full of anger and trauma, and some certainly do. However, there are also people who are profoundly and creatively changed as a direct result of their captivity: one decided to mend his marriage, another decided to put his business on a more honest footing and another, a pleasure-bound journalist, returned to the Church and started to go on retreat regularly – much to the bewilderment of his family! It was as if they were able to discover themselves more or perhaps were forced to jettison parts of themselves that they had learnt they did not need or want. In religious terms these people went through a 'stripping', their lives reduced to the essentials. They were forced to spend time in these constrained circumstances, shorn of distractions, and it made them question who they were and what they actually wanted from life. They discovered that the 'stripping' they experienced enabled them to choose to become more real, more connected, more themselves. The experiences jolted them awake.[1]

These two examples of being stripped through illness and loss of freedom chime in with the earlier chapters in this book about the stripping away caused by suffering and death. However, it is not inevitable that being woken in this way will lead to people making changes in their lives; I think of the 33 Chilean miners who were imprisoned underground for 69 long days in 2010. Many promised themselves and often God that they would be totally different people if they could emerge alive. They promised to be better husbands and better fathers, better people. No doubt they meant it, stuck in the belly of the earth stripped of their normal lives. However, the reality on their return proved more complex and painful. Although some of the miners did change, some have struggled and slipped back into their old lives and failed to fulfil their promises to themselves and others. Being woken up from our sleepwalking in life guarantees nothing in itself; it just offers an opportunity we can take up or turn down. I hate mornings, as I mentioned in the first chapter, so yesterday, when my alarm went off, I hit the snooze button. It rang six times and I hit the snooze button six times. It then gave up and I went soundly back to sleep, making myself late for a meeting. Hopeless! Being woken up is being offered a choice but the outcome is not assured unless we are prepared to stay with it and work with it.

In Deuteronomy chapter 30, Moses puts the following challenge before the people:

> I call heaven and earth to witness against you today: I place before you life and death, blessing and curse. Choose life so that you and your children shall live.[2]

Well, we might assume that any fool would know to choose life but mostly we don't choose to be fully alive. Jesus says: 'I am come that they might have life, and that they may have it abundantly.'[3] We so often choose not to live life abundantly. We habitually suppress a great deal of our own sensitivity and unconsciously train our children from an early age to do likewise. Why would we choose to limit ourselves in this way? Because typically the choices are hard: it is not possible, for example, to develop the ability to see beauty without also being able to see ugliness. It is not possible to develop the capacity to experience great joy without experiencing great sadness. We soon discover in life that any increase in our openness to see what is lovely increases our openness to being hurt. This is a very real dilemma of human living. We cannot just choose an abundant happy life even though the lie of our culture is to promise that we can. The choice is actually much starker. It is between a life which is closed down to change, defended, narrow and me-centred (with the likelihood that this will mostly not be intolerably painful) or a life which is able to take the risk of change, is open, generous and compassionate, which will bring a vast increase in delight, but also in pain and hurt.

Shirley, the Liverpool housewife in the film *Shirley Valentine*, when faced with this realisation, says this:

> What I kept thinking about was how I'd lived such a *little* life. And one way or another even that would be over pretty soon. I thought to myself, my life has been a crime really ... a crime against God. Because ... I didn't live it fully. I'd allowed myself to live this little life when inside me was so much more. So much more that I could have lived a bigger life with – but it has all gone unused, and now it never will be.[4]

To live life abundantly is Jesus' invitation to us; live, don't sleepwalk through life, it is not why we have been created. Probably (though it would be difficult to choose just one) my favourite novel is *Gilead* by Marilynne

Robinson, a mesmerising novel full of wisdom and tenderness. In it the key character says, 'There are a thousand, thousand reasons to live, every one of them sufficient.'[5] Our lives are full of grace.

However, there is always a huge temptation to retreat into unreality. I love this poem, 'The Optimist' by D. H. Lawrence:

> The optimist builds himself
> Safe inside a cell,
> And paints the walls, sky blue
> And blocks up the door
> And says he is in heaven.[6]

An excellent example of sleepwalking! God has absolutely no interest in the optimistic but unrealistic cells we build to protect ourselves: our material possessions, our status, our abilities, our families and our successes. Lives we construct limiting ourselves to a reality which is in our comfort zone and closed to the bigger reality of God. So clearly God is content for our sky blue painted cells to be knocked down and as life proceeds they surely will be. God's concern is to let the real sunlight stream in and more importantly to make it possible for us to get out! We can be freed from our small hopes and ambitions so that we can begin to hope more extravagantly for and with God. We need to see and engage with God's reality, not our constructed human reality. We, of course, always have the choice to rebuild and to barricade ourselves back into our sky blue painted cell and all too often, perhaps through fear or laziness, we do just that.

C. S. Lewis is a very well respected Christian writer to whom many of us turn for answers to life's hard questions. He experienced just such a knocking down, in the case of his logical, well-argued and secure Christian faith. He discovered that his well-honed arguments did not entirely hold up in the light of life's events. At the relatively late age of 45 Lewis married for the first time and found his cosy bachelor shell cracked open by his love for Joy Davidman. Tragically, what had been cracked open by love was then totally shattered by Joy's illness and her all too early death. In his powerful book A *Grief Observed*, he shared with great honesty how this suffering and death had knocked down all that he had built: 'If my house has collapsed at one blow, that is because it was a house of cards ... If I had really cared, as I thought I did, about the sorrows of the world, I should not have been overwhelmed when my own sorrow came.' [7]

Being stripped back is not the only way in which we are awoken from sleepwalking. We are also awoken by those experiences which extend, enhance and bless us. I have written earlier about love and about wonder, but while 'stripping' at least gets our attention we can all too often take joy and gift for granted; gratitude is so important. Henry Ward Beecher writes:

There are joys which long to be ours ... which come about us like birds seeking inlet; but we are shut up to them, and so they bring us nothing, but sit a while upon the roof, and then fly away. [8]

Life is so full of joys and gifts. This failure to recognise and receive gifts often happens because we set our minds too firmly upon what we think we want and need and are not open to other things; what we think will bring us joy. I experienced an example of this when I moved from our first married home. I had been very happy in Lincolnshire and had close friends whom I did not want to leave. We moved a long way south to Kent and when we got there, in a way, I was looking for the same friends again. As I met with new people offering friendship I couldn't see who they were or what they were offering me because I was looking for the friends I had just left behind. Of course I didn't find them in Kent as they were still living in Lincolnshire! It took me ages to see the gift of the wonderful friends who were there for me in Kent and to engage with them properly. I had blocked myself from seeing the new friends I had been given because I only wanted what I had just left behind. I was not open to these new gifts. I regretted the lack of time to enjoy those new friendships and the time I had wasted, and as we moved on to Oxford I did not make the same mistake again. I was open to the gift of friendship in whatever form it might arrive and wonderfully I have discovered that it is always different every time.

It is strange how much we often want things to be the same. It takes a long time for most of us to grasp that our lives are always changing. We often convince ourselves that only in unchanging stability can we find happiness but in fact the opposite may well be true. If we insist that happiness derives from things staying the same, this very insistence can make us miserable because it simply is not the truth. Life is always moving us on and wisdom lies in recognising what the late Brother Roger of Taizé so memorably called 'the dynamic of the provisional'.

So, however we might like it to be, life relentlessly and wonderfully wakes us up offering us many a possible foothold in reality. However, the key issue is not actually what is happening in our lives on the outside but what is happening to us on the inside, even if this is not what we feel. Every time we are woken from our sleepwalking we are offered the opportunity to know the reality of ourselves better. This is an essential part of our journey to being more fully alive. This inner journey can be painful and is often laborious. In my nearly 60 years on earth I wish I could tell you that my inner journey has been onwards and upwards but to be truthful it has been up and down, forwards and backwards and quite often round and round. I often think I am following the thread of myself and then find I have lost it again. There is a sense I have in life that I am always being brought back to the beginning.

This process is not helped by the illusions we like to project about ourselves; when we are face to face with the gap between our lives and the reality of being seen and known by God. Part of knowing ourselves is inevitably that we come face to face with sin; indeed we need to wake up to our sinfulness to have any possibility of growing into our real, best selves. Sin, in the terms of this book, is about seeing the gap between how we live and God's reality and dealing with it, about recognising how we are living against the grain. An 'awake' sinner is someone who is beginning to grasp that they are living in a bigger world than they can see; their familiar world is not all that is to be reckoned with. As Rowan Williams writes: 'A sinner who has woken up is someone who knows that he has some learning to do.'[9]

Time and again I find that I am capable of choosing against such learning and against becoming more alive and more whole which is why my life's journey so often seems to bring me round full circle. I shall never forget my long-suffering counsellor Gordon gently and patiently, as I was blurting out in frustration and anger some issue, asking if I recognised the place in which I found myself: 'It's similar to before', he pointed out, and metaphorically took me by the hand and walked me around it again. 'Do you recognise it?' Actually although life often brings us back to the same issues, I think it is more like a spiral than a circle because it does not quite bring us back to the same place. So what will I do with the opportunity of change and growth this time?

I see so many things in myself, and in the people I have the privilege of listening to, which block change and growth. I will nod to just a few! Well, denial is a good starting place: surely what I have seen about myself cannot be true! There is also fear: if I live differently what will it be like; what will the consequences be for me? In me there is also not a little cowardice and laziness and this mixed in with greed: there always seems to be some sort of reward in living my life badly. So, if we are not careful our lives can be a constant evasion of our true selves.

We have to take responsibility either for using these waking-up experiences to bring us to life or for walking away, slipping back into our sleepwalking. If we don't we are at risk of letting life live us rather than us live life. No one can do it for us, no one can force us and we cannot force another. In *Zorba the Greek*, Nikos Kazantzakis tells a story about how attempting to force something on can do real harm:

> One morning ... I discovered a cocoon in the bark of a tree, just as the butterfly was making a hole in the case preparing to come out. I waited a while, but it was too long appearing and I was impatient. I bent over it and breathed on it to warm it up. I warmed it as quickly as I could and the miracle began to happen before my eyes, faster than life. The case opened, the butterfly started slowly crawling out and I shall never forget my horror when I saw how its wings were folded back and crumpled; the wretched butterfly tried with its whole body to unfold them. Bending over it I tried to help with my hands. In vain.
>
> It needed to be hatched out patiently and the unfolding of the wings should be a gradual process in the sun. Now it was too late. My breath had forced the butterfly to appear all crumpled, before its time. It struggled desperately and, a few seconds later, died in the palm of my hand.[10]

So we need to learn to be patient with others and with ourselves. I used to say to trainee clergy that one of the most demanding acts of love is to accompany another as they struggle to change; to keep faith with them and stay with them in what is often a long and sometimes tedious journey. Fortunately and crucially we have an infinitely patient and loving God. The key to all of this is not to separate the two aspects of our spiritual journey. We have been thinking about knowing ourselves better but if this is done with little attention to knowing God the consequence could be that we despair; that knowing ourselves, really knowing ourselves, we are at a loss about what to do. On the other hand if we were simply to try to know God better without knowing ourselves then it could lead to great arrogance.

Jesus is the most accessible way in which we can begin to understand and know God. As Michael Ramsey put it, 'in God there is no unChristlikeness at all'. So Jesus shows us God but also shows us how to be fully human. Jesus was profoundly alive himself; always dancing to the kingdom's tune and this constantly caused him to be at odds with people. He was always running into trouble with the Pharisees and the teachers of the law and his encounter in Luke 13[11] with a crippled woman finds Jesus and the religious authorities in yet another stand-off. The tension is palpable; Jesus now has a following and all eyes are on him as he teaches in the synagogue.

Let's imagine the scene. It's another set piece. On the one hand the synagogue leader, just waiting for a chance to get the latest indiscretion out to the authorities, and on the other hand the disciples trying to take in this extraordinary man so full of life, so utterly and bewilderingly awake. The focus of all their attention is the woman, bent double, not even able to look up. She has been suffering with this terrible affliction for 18 years. What will Jesus do? Will he set the woman free or will he play safe? He breaks the rules, calls the woman forward, lays his hands on her and says, 'You are rid of your trouble.' 'Woman, you are free.' Immediately the woman straightens up and starts to praise God.

Jesus waits for the inevitable confrontation and it is not slow in coming. The president of the synagogue is indignant and fears that the people are there just to hear Jesus and to watch him healing people. He says, 'Six days have been defined as working days. Come on one of them if you want to be healed, not on the Sabbath.' (You can almost hear him saying, 'You've been ill for 18 years, one more day won't make any difference!') The tension is almost palpable as Jesus calmly steps forward to take him on. 'You hypocrites … all of you would think nothing of untying your ox or your donkey from its stall on the Sabbath to take it to the water to drink. So why isn't it all right to untie this poor woman from her bonds by which she has been tied for 18 long years?' At this his opponents were covered with confusion and the people were delighted at the wonderful things he was doing.

Jesus as always is living out of the kingdom perspective; opening up a reality which is astonishing and challenging. Things look so different from where he stands. That was the problem for the religious authorities and they were threatened because they were the movers and shakers with the most to lose. They had life arranged to suit themselves. They had compromised their religious beliefs with the world's reality; the world's domination systems and they certainly weren't expecting or wanting God to do a new thing, except on their own terms. God, though, is committed to life, giving life, saving life, enriching life, restoring life, fulfilling life. Through the life of Jesus we too are challenged to start to see things differently; to see them from God's point of view. We are invited to share in God's life-giving enterprise and we have to decide many times a week whether we choose life or death. We can choose to speak up for those with no voice, to preserve the environment, to act ethically, to care for victims, to build community, to save life, or we can choose to watch our own backs, compromise on the truth, misuse the earth's resources, collude with the powerful, step on others and destroy life. And don't think the Church is exempt from this choice. Churches often say they are following Christ, but choose to do things which bring more death than life to themselves and others. Certainly to live a religious life is no safeguard. As J. V. Taylor once wrote:

It has long been my conviction that God is not hugely interested as to whether we are religious or not. What matters, and matters supremely, is whether we are alive or not. If your religion brings you fully to life God will be in it; but if your religion inhibits your capacity for life or makes you run away from it, you may be sure that God is against it, just as Jesus was.[12]

Jesus showed throughout his ministry just how costly it is to live an awake, really alive life and in the end it cost him everything. It cost him his life. The crucifixion seemed to be the ultimate moment when the world's addiction to unreality won and death trumped life, but as we know this was not the last word. God's power for life will not be overridden, resisted or defeated. Through the resurrection, God's reality triumphs and the cycle of death is broken; the resurrection is not some future speculation but brings life to us now.

The God of life wills life for us and is with us in all the complexity of our living. In this book I have tried to explore some of the ways in which we can listen more closely to our lives and grasp the opportunities which come our way to try to live out of a different kind of reality. God's reality breaks into our lives, waking us up and challenging our unwillingness to receive new life. We have been created to be fully alive, to live out of the deepest part of ourselves and in Christ to become our real, best selves. We don't want to come to death to discover we have not lived. As Mary Oliver writes, 'I don't want to end up simply having visited this world.'[13] At the resurrection the disciples proclaimed to their complete bewilderment 'He is alive!'. As they looked back they saw that 'alive' was what Jesus had always been: alive in himself and totally alive to God. John's Gospel sums it up in one deeply profound sentence: 'In him was life and that life was the light of all people.'[14]

and that will be heaven

and that will be heaven
at last the first unclouded
seeing

to stand like the sunflower
turned full face to the sun drenched
with light in the still centre
held while the circling planets
hum with an utter joy

seeing and knowing
at last in every particle
seen and known and not turning
away

never turning away
again[5]

FOR DISCUSSION

1. This chapter gives two examples of being 'stripped' through illness and loss of freedom. Have you experienced anything similar in your life?

2. 'Being woken up from sleepwalking in life guarantees nothing in itself' (p.105). Does the image of an alarm clock on permanent 'snooze' challenge you in any way?

3. Why do we often not choose to be fully alive? How do you respond to what the author says about this on p. 105?

4. Are you aware in your own life of ways in which as the Shirley Valentine character says, 'I'd lived such a little life'?

5. What 'sky blue painted cells' have we built for ourselves?

6. Are there gifts and joys which you are taking for granted or refusing to acknowledge?

7. How do we respond to change? Is Brother Roger of Taizé's memorable phrase 'the dynamic of the provisional' helpful?

8. How do you respond to the description of sin on p.111? Do you find it helpful? Truthful?

9. How do you react to the list of things which are blocks to change (p.111) Do you have any other ideas?

10. How do you respond to the idea that knowing ourselves better without knowing God better can lead to despair and knowing God better without knowing ourselves better can lead to great arrogance? (p.113)

BIBLE PASSAGE FOR
REFLECTION: LUKE 13:10-17

1. By healing the woman, Jesus breaks the rules. Are there rules which we should be challenging in the Church or in the world?
2. Jesus says, 'Woman you are free.' From what do you need to be freed?
3. How has the Church compromised its beliefs and behaviour in its relationship with the world's reality, values and power?
4. What does choosing between life and death look like in your context?
5. Does your religion bring you more fully alive?

CLOSING PRAYER

O Living God,
we who are partly living,
scarcely hoping,
and fitfully caring,
pray to you now
to make us fully alive.
Give us the vitality, awareness and commitment
that we see in Jesus Christ,
through the power of his death and resurrection.
We ask this in his name.
Amen.

J.V. Taylor, *A Matter of Life and Death*
(SCM Press, 1986), p.33

NOTES

CHAPTER 1: A KIND OF SLEEPWALKING

1. Henry Thoreau, *Walden*, New American Library, 1960, p.65.
2. Thomas Merton, quoted in Robert Ellsberg, *The Saints' Guide to Happiness*, DLT, 2004, p.186.
3. Francis Dewar, *Invitations: God's Calling for Everyone*, SPCK, 1996, p.97.
4. Helene Cixous and Mireille Calle Gruber, *Rootprints: Memory and Life Writing*, Routledge, 1997, p.8.
5. *The Comedy of Dante Alighieri, the Florentine, Cantica 1, Hell*, trans Dorothy L. Sayers, Canto I, i-iii, p.71.
6. Paul Eluard, quoted in *This Sunrise of Wonder*, Michael Mayne, DLT, 2008, p.67.
7. Luke 7:36-50.
8. Carol Ann Duffy, 'Homesick', *Selling Manhattan*, Anvil Press, 1987.

CHAPTER 2: WAKING UP TO SUFFERING

1. George Fox, *Journal*, revised edition by John Nickalls, Religious Society of Friends, 1975.
2. Ellsberg, *The Saints' Guide to Happiness*, p.134.
3. Henri Nouwen, *Can You Drink the Cup?* Ave Maria Press, 1996, p.134.
4. John O'Donohue, *Eternal Echoes*, Bantam Press, 2000, p.232.
5. Quoted in Mark Barrett, *Crossing*, DLT, 2001, p.20.

6. Benedicta Ward, *Songs of the Desert Fathers*, Mowbray, 1975, p.139.

7. Diadochos of Photiki, *The Philokalia,* vol. I, p.291.

8. Ellsberg, *The Saints' Guide to Happiness,* p.109-110.

9. Leon Bloy, *Pilgrim of the Absolute,* ed. Raissa Maritain, Pantheon, 1947, p.349.

10. Informed by Ellsberg, *The Saints' Guide to Happiness*, p.121.

11. Luke 8:22-25.

12. John 13:6-9.

13. Matthew 26:69-75.

14. Luke 22:3.

15. Ellsberg, *The Saints' Guide to Happiness,* p.122-3.

16. Job 42:3 NIV.

17. Romans 8:37-39.

18. Sermon preached at St John's College.

19. George Herbert, 'Bitter-Sweet', *The English Poems of George Herbert,* ed C. A Tatrides, J M Dent, 1974, p.176.

CHAPTER 3: WAKING UP TO WONDER

1. J. V. Taylor, *A Matter of Life and Death,* SCM Press, 1986, p.8.

2. Edwin Muir, 'The Labyrinth', *Collected Poems,* Faber and Faber, 1960, p.65.

3. Mary Oliver, 'Messenger', *Thirst,* Beacon Press, 2004, p.1.

4. Mayne, *This Sunrise of Wonder,* p.295.

5. Graham Swift, *Ever After,* Picador, 1992, p.71.

6. Dennis Potter, interview with Melvyn Bragg, Channel 4, 15 March 1994.

7. Taylor, *A Matter of Life and Death,* p.28.

8. Emily Dickinson, 'The only news I know', *The Complete Poems,* Faber and Faber, 1970, p.401.

9. Thomas W. Ogletree, *Hospitality to the Stranger,* Fortress Press, 1985, p.2-3.

10. Thomas Merton, *Confessions of a Guilty Bystander,* Sheldon Press, 1977, p.153.

11. Matthew 17:1-13.

12. Luke 9:18-20.
13. Matthew 17:4.
14. With thanks to Revd John McManners.
15. Veronica Zundel, 'Song', first published in *Faith in Her Words*, Lion, 1991.

CHAPTER 4: WAKING UP TO DEATH
1. Lepp.
2. Ellsberg, *The Saints' Guide to Happiness*, p.138.
3. Mark Haddon, *A Spot of Bother*, Jonathan Cape, 2006, p.4.
4. James Runcie, *Canvey Island*, Bloomsbury, 2006, p.5
5. Dietrich Bonhoeffer, quoted in J. Martin Bailey and Douglass Gilbert, *The Steps of Bonhoeffer*, Macmillan, 1969, p.73.
6. Cardinal Bernardin, quoted in Ellsberg, *The Saints' Guide to Happiness*, 2004.
7. Ellsberg, *The Saints' Guide to Happiness*, p.145.
8. Dag Hammarskjöld, *Markings*, Faber and Faber, 1997, p.99.
9. Barrett, *Crossing*, p.106.
10. Nicholas Wolterstorff, *Lament for a Son*, SPCK, 1997, p.15.
11. Martin Luther King, *Strength to Love*, Fortress Press, 1981, p.113.
12. Philippians 1:20-24.
13. Revelations 7:16-17.
14. Mary Oliver, 'In Blackwater Woods', from *American Primitive*, used by permission of Little, Brown and Company.
15. Norman MacCaig, 'Small Boy', taken from *Collected Poems*, Birlinn Books, 2009.
16. Informed by Ellsberg, *The Saints' Guide to Happiness*, p.146-151.
17. Elizabeth Jennings, extracts from 'Into the Hour', *Moments of Grace*, Carcanet, 1979, p.7.

CHAPTER 5: WAKING UP TO LOVE

1. William Blake, 'The Little Black Boy', *The Works of William Blake*, Wordsworth editions, 1994, p. 58.

2. Wendy Cope, 'Valentine', *Serious Concerns*, Faber and Faber, 1992, p.12.

3. David Ford, *The Shape of Living*, Zondervan, 2002, p.8.

4. Micheal O'Siadhail, 'Out of the Blue', *Collected Poems*, Bloodaxe, 2013.

5. Louis de Bernières, *Captain Corelli's Mandolin*, Vintage, 1999, p.345.

6. 1 Corinthians 13:4-7, NIV.

7. Matthew 25:35-36, NIV.

8. Joan Chittister, *For Everything a Season*, Orbis, 2013, p. 42.

9. John O'Donohue, *Divine Beauty*, Bantam Press, 2003, p.174.

10. W.H. Vanstone, *Love's Endeavour, Love's Expense*, DLT, 1977.

11. Mark 12:31 NIV.

12. Martin L. Smith, *Nativities and Passions*, DLT, 1996, p.188.

13. George Herbert, 'Love', *The English Poems of George Herbert*, ed. C. A. Tatrides, J M Dent, 1974, p.192.

14. Thomas Merton, *The Seven Storey Mountain*, Harcourt, Brace and Co, 1977, p.200.

15. R. S. Thomas, 'The Kingdom', *Collected Poems 1945 - 1990*, J. M. Dent, 1993.

16. Luke: 15:11-32. NIV.

17. Matthew 20:1-16.

18. Trevor Dennis, 'God's Forgiveness', *Speaking of God*, SPCK, 1992, p.91.

19. Julian of Norwich, *Enfolded in Love*, DLT, 1994, p.46.

CHAPTER 6: WAKING UP TO LIFE

1. Melvyn Matthews, *Nearer than Breathing*, SPCK, 2002, p.55-6.

2. Deuteronomy 30:19, Eugene H. Peterson, *The Message*, Think Books, 2003.

3. John 10:10, NIV.
4. Willy Russell, *Shirley Valentine,* Methuen, 1993, p.30 (slightly adapted).
5. Marilynne Robinson, *Gilead,* Virago, 2004, p.277.
6. D. H. Lawrence, 'The Optimist', quoted in Hugh Rayment-Pickard, *The Myths of Time: From St Augustine to American Beauty,* DLT, 2004, p.xi.
7. C. S. Lewis, *A Grief Observed,* Faber and Faber, 1961, p.43.
8. Henry Ward Beecher, quoted in Joan Chittister, *For Everything a Season,* Orbis Books, 2013, p.16.
9. Rowan Williams and Joan Chittister, *For All That Has Been, Thanks,* Canterbury Press, 2010, p.58.
10. Nikos Kazantzakis, *Zorba the Greek,* Simon and Schuster, 1952, p.120-1.
11. Luke 13:10-17.
12. J. V. Taylor, *A Matter of Life and Death,* SCM Press, 1986, p.18.
13. Mary Oliver, 'When death comes', *New and Selected Poems,* Beacon Press, 1993.
14. John 1:4.
15. Evangeline Paterson, 'And that will be heaven', in Mary Batchelor (ed), *The Lion Book of Christian Poetry,* Lion, 2005.

Thanks are due to the following for permission to quote copyright material:

Angela Ashwin and Zondervan for prayer from *The Book of a Thousand Prayers* by Angela Ashwin;

Anvil Press for 'Homesick' taken from *Selling Manhattan* by Carol Ann Duffy published by Anvil Press Poetry in 1987;

Beacon Press for 'Messenger' from the volume *Thirst* by Mary Oliver, published by Beacon Press, Boston, Copyright © 2004 by Mary Oliver, used herewith by permission of the Charlotte Sheedy Literary Agency, Inc;

Birlinn Books for 'Small Boy' taken from *Collected Poems* by Norman MacCaig;

Bloodaxe Books for extract from *Poems* by Micheal O'Siadhail (Bloodaxe Books, 2013);

Carolyn Rowland-Jones for 'And That Will Be Heaven' by Evangeline Paterson, used by permission;

David Higham for 'Into the Hour' from *Collected Poems* by Elizabeth Jennings (Carcanet Press, new edition, 2012);

'Valentine' taken from *Serious Concerns* © Wendy Cope and reprinted by permission of Faber and Faber Ltd;

Extract taken from 'The Labyrinth' taken from *Collected Poems* © Estate of Edwin Muir and reprinted by permission of Faber and Faber Ltd;

SCM Press for John V. Taylor, *A Matter of Life and Death*, SCM Press 1986, pp. 18, 33. Used by permission of the estate of the late John V. Taylor;

SPCK for extracts from *Speaking of God* by Trevor Dennis (SPCK, 1992) and from *All Desires Known* by Janet Morley (SPCK, 1992);

Richard Harries for his prayer, taken from *Praying Round the Clock* (Continuum, 1983);

Taylor and Francis for *Rootprints – Memory and Life Writing* by Helene Cixous and Mireille Calle Gruber (Routledge, 1997);

Hymns Ancient and Modern Ltd for *Letters and Papers from Prison* by Dietrich Bonhoeffer;

Little, Brown and Company for 'In Blackwater Woods' from *American Primitive* by Mary Oliver, copyright © 1978, 1979, 1980, 1981, 1982, 1983 by Mary Oliver; by permission of Little, Brown and Company. All rights reserved;

Orion Publishing Group for 'The Kingdom' by R S Thomas, taken from *Collected Poems 1945 – 1990* by R S Thomas © 1993 by R S Thomas;

Veronica Zundel for her poem 'Song', first published in *Faith in her Words* (Lion, 1991).